The Authorities
Powerful Wisdom from Leaders in the Field

MADELINE ELBIRT

Award-Winning Author

Copyright © 2021 Authorities Press

ISBN: 978-1-77277-448-1

All rights reserved. No portion of this book may be reproduced mechanically, electronically, or by any other means, including photocopying, without permission of the publisher or author except in the case of brief quotations embodied in critical articles and reviews. It is illegal to copy this book, post it to a website, or distribute it by any other means without permission from the publisher or author.

Limits of Liability and Disclaimer of Warranty
The author and publisher shall not be liable for your misuse of the enclosed material. This book is strictly for informational and educational purposes.

Warning – Disclaimer
The purpose of this book is to educate and entertain. The author and/or publisher do not guarantee that anyone following these techniques, suggestions, tips, ideas, or strategies will become successful. The author and/or publisher shall have neither liability nor responsibility to anyone with respect to any loss or damage caused, or alleged to be caused, directly or indirectly by the information contained in this book.

Medical Disclaimer
The medical or health information in this book is provided as an information resource only, and is not to be used or relied on for any diagnostic or treatment purposes. This information is not intended to be patient education, does not create any patient-physician relationship, and should not be used as a substitute for professional diagnosis and treatment.

Publisher
Authorities Press
Markham, ON
Canada

Printed in the United States, Canada, and the United Kingdom.

FOREWORD

Experts are to be admired for their knowledge, but they often remain unrecognized by the general public because they save their information and insights for paying customers and clients. There are many experts in a given field, but their impact is limited to the handful of people with whom they work.

Unlike experts, authorities share their knowledge and expertise far more broadly, so they make a big impact on the world. Authorities become known and admired as leading experts and, as such, typically do very well economically and professionally. Most authorities are also mature enough to know that part of the joy of monetary success is the accompanying moral and spiritual obligation to give back.

Many people want to learn and work with well-respected and generous authorities, but don't always know where to find them. They may be known to their peers, or within a specific community, but have not had the opportunity to reach a wider audience. At one time, they might have submitted a proposal to the *For Dummies* or *Chicken Soup for the Soul* series of books, but it's now almost impossible to get accepted as a new author in such a branded book series.

It is more than fitting that Raymond Aaron, an internationally known and respected authority in his own right, would be the one to recognize the need for a new venue in which authorities could share their considerable knowledge with readers everywhere. As the only author ever to be included in both of the book series mentioned above, Raymond has had the opportunity to give back and he understands how crucial it is for authorities to have a platform from which to share their expertise.

I have known and worked with Raymond for a number of years and consider him a valued friend and talented coach. He knows how to spot talented and knowledgeable people and he desires to see them prosper. Over the years, success coaching and speaking engagements around the world have made it possible for Raymond to meet many of these talented authorities. He recognizes and relates to their passion and enthusiasm for what they do, as well as their desire to share what they know. He tells me that's why he created this new nonfiction branded book series, *The Authorities*.

Dr. Nido Qubein
President, High Point University

TABLE OF CONTENTS

Foreword i

Introduction v

The Truth About Romance Scams 1
Madeline Elbirt

The Woman of my Dreams and a Million Dollars 17
Raymond Aaron

Happiness: How to Experience the "Real Deals" 21
Marci Shimoff

Sex, Love and Relationships 29
Dr. John Gray

Unleashing Your Full Potential 35
Brian Tracy

Exceeding Expectations While Building Long-Term Relationships 45
Alice Madisha & Jannie Smith

Save My Relationship 55
Chris Hart

Romancing Your Way Through Network Marketing 65
Dorcas Tay

Enter Into a Passionate Relationship with Your Own Life .. 75
Silvana Avram

The Love Drug 91
Wilma David Aguila

Single Again? 113
Linda J. Levesque

Bringing Balance to Your LifeMy Journey to Purpose 129
Dennis Garrido

INTRODUCTION

Welcome to *The Authorities*. It is an anthology of stories and ideas from individuals who have distinguished themselves in life and business. They are people who leave a big footprint on the world, and as leaders in their particular fields, they also understand the importance and obligation of giving something back.

Authorities are not just experts. They are also known to be outstanding in their fields and their communities. Because of this important difference, authorities can contribute more to humanity through their chosen work and giving back. You will recognize some of *The Authorities* in this book, especially since some are world-famous. Others, whom you may not yet know of, are just as exceptional.

The featured author is Madeline Elbirt. As the internet has become woven into our lives, scammers have begun to use it to target unsuspecting individuals. Nowhere is this more evident than in romantic scams. Madeline Elbirt knows about these scams. She has done her homework, after being scammed years ago. Now she shares these scammers' tricks with you in *The Truth About Romance Scams!*

Madeline breaks down the stories that scammers use to lure you in. She also outlines some common red flags that can help you to avoid being a victim. Filled with examples of real-life stories straight from the scammers, Madeline helps you to avoid falling for these schemes, with practical wisdom.

Along the way, she encourages you to share your story to help others to feel less alone if they have been victims of one of these scams. Madeline also points out how important it is to share this information with friends and family to help them avoid these scams as well.

Not only does Madeline give you practical information regarding what these scams look like, she also shares what motivates scammers. Ultimately, if you want to avoid being a victim of romantic scammers, *The Truth About Romance Scams* is the guide you have been looking for!

To be considered for a subsequent edition of *The Authorities*, please go to www.aaron.com.

The Truth About Romance Scams

MADELINE ELBIRT

These days, it seems that scams have integrated themselves into every aspect of our lives. During the pandemic, as more individuals use social media to connect with others, these scams have only increased. While all these scams can end up costing you money or time, romantic ones can end up costing you emotionally, mentally, and financially.

Unfortunately, once we have fallen for one of these scams, it is hard to admit that you have been duped. There is a sense of shame. I understand how you feel because I have been there. In this chapter, I am revealing my story for the first time, along with tips to determine if you are connecting with a real person or a scammer on your favorite dating app.

You may find some of these stories to be ridiculous and even funny, but most of them are sad and cruel. I will teach you the tricks scammers play, and show you the things you can do to discover their real identity, exposing the scam itself.

How does a romantic scam begin? A person goes onto a dating site or Facebook, where they get an online message from someone unknown to them. They might check out their profile and picture before answering. A conversation begins by text. You might honestly think you are talking to the person in the profile, but in reality that image was stolen. The scammer has created a fake profile, meant to lure you in.

In this day and age, scammers are not specifically targeting men or women. That fake profile is likely one of several, each crafted to target specific individuals.

The scammer starts out with lots of compliments, meant to romance you with loving words that get you emotionally invested. Within a short time, they tell you they are falling in love with you. It is all about being charming before they first ask you for cash. As you chat, they might suggest you leave the dating site or Facebook for Hangouts or Whatsapp. The move is meant to limit anyone's ability to track them later.

Some scammers will carry on with you for a month or more to get your trust before even mentioning money. During that time, they are building a level of trust, telling you one of a million stories that circulate among the scammers. You might even receive long written letters or passages, telling you about themselves, what they want in a loving partner, and their struggles. All of these are meant to play upon your sympathy and get you off your guard. These stories are written by a literate person or borrowed passages from books. Nothing about the relationship between the two of you is genuine, but they are clever, so you don't realize it.

If you think you are alone in being duped, you aren't. These scams are being perpetrated by third world people looking to cash in on first world countries' citizens and their comparatively rich lives, and they are happening every minute. There is no feeling of guilt, just a focus on doing whatever it takes to get you to send money.

Romance scams are costing people their life savings, homes, cars, and even their lives. People are left with nothing, while their scammer is buying expensive watches, cars, and other luxury items with the money they have stolen.

We know that many people in third world countries are desperately poor, living under the illusion that first world citizens are all rich, so they can afford to lose some of that cash, but this does not condone the harm they are causing their victims.

Romance scams affect men and woman who are looking to meet someone for friendship or love. The scams originated in Nigeria, but they have been picked up by countries throughout the world. Young boys and girls are attempting to steal money by professing love for their victim. It is heartbreaking and cruel!

These scams are being perpetrated by young African, Indian, and Caribbean boys and girls from third world countries. The majority of scammers are young people between 18 and 26 years of age. They call themselves Yahoo boys. They are often working many victims simultaneously.

Sitting on the floor of a room, these young people all have computers, probably rented, so that they are difficult to trace. They share or sell information with each other, allowing for different scammers to get funds from the same people over and over.

I saw a video of young African men being interviewed by a U.S. reporter. The reporter asked, "Don't they feel bad about stealing money from people?" They answered, "No, because they have lots of money and we need it." When asked if they realized they were committing a crime, they said, "It isn't a crime because it's on the internet!" This is the logic of a scammer!

Scammers are becoming more sophisticated, as this grows into a viable business for people around the world.

There is a true story of a woman in Vancouver who spoke with a man on a dating site for 2 years. He romanced her, said he loved her and wanted to come and marry her. But instead of landing at the airport in Canada, he kept giving her excuses and asked for more money. She was so in love with him that she gave him almost a million dollars! Her daughter found out what her mom was doing, and that the man was a scammer. She proved it to her mom. The emotional toll of finding out she had been duped drove the mother to commit suicide.

Many people would say, "How could she be so stupid to give her money to someone she never even met?"

These scammers can be persistent, convincing, and charming. It is easy, if their victim is alone and very vulnerable, for them to craft a story that will get them emotionally involved, thus making it easier to get them to hand over their cash.

I understand how this could happen because I have been a victim of these scammers. At the time, I was widowed, alone, and very vulnerable. After a few years of widowhood, the loneliness became unbearable. I wanted someone who I could love and share my life with. The challenge was that I don't go to bars or know a lot of available men. Like so many others, I turned to a dating site. There I met a man who charmed me and said all the right things. He told me he was Swedish, widowed, and living in a city not far from me. After talking via the app, he asked me to go to dinner with him the next week. I was so excited and tried on a dozen outfits, my head filled with nervous anticipation.

Then he said he was an architect/engineer and had been bidding on a contract in Cyprus to construct a shopping mall. He shared the details of his proposal with me and I supported him. The Friday before our date he told me he was presenting his project. I cheered him on. We had become friends, talking about our losses, what we wanted in our future, our families, and plans for the future.

He called me Saturday morning to tell me he had won the project and had to fly to New York to meet with the owners and sign all the paperwork. Then he cancelled our date. The project was to last two months, but he said he would call or text me every day. Throughout that time, he did keep in touch with me, telling me how the project was going and sending me pictures of Cyprus taken on his one day off. We continued to plan our future together. It sounds great, doesn't it? Yet, all this emotion had been stoked without me ever laying eyes on him.

One day he said he needed my help. He wanted me to go to the Apple store for some items. He sent me a list of technical jargon that I didn't understand. I am not a tech expert.

I went to the store and asked them if they had what he had written, assuming it was a manual of some sort. It turned out to be three Apple computers that amounted to $9,000.00! I called him immediately and told him the cost. He told me he needed them to finish his project so he could come home to me sooner. He said he would pay me back as soon as he returned. I relented and paid for the computers and shipped them. It totaled $9,500. He was so grateful!

Two months turned into three and then he told me he was finally coming home and asked me to pick him up at the airport. He sent me his flight information on what looked like a legitimate airline manifest. As he was supposedly driving to the airport, he called to say he couldn't wait to see me. He was due to return on Sunday. On Sunday morning, I got a call from his phone but with someone else's voice. He said he was holding my friend for non-payment of duties on equipment he had shipped in for the job. He said he would give my friend his phone back later.

My friend sent me a picture of a newspaper article which mentioned his name and the arrest. I was suspicious and went on a Cyprus website about customs duties. It said they did not hold people who didn't pay duties but allowed them to pay when they got home.

My "friend" called me the next day. By now, I knew he was trying to scam me. I was heartbroken and furious at him. He explained that he couldn't leave Cyprus and needed $25,000 Euros to come home to me. I told him that was too bad, I didn't care, and that I knew he was a liar and a scammer. He continued to try to change my mind, even saying the money would get him home to me and the kids. What kids? He didn't have any and mine were grown and gone. He was also trying to scam another woman who had kids and he had gotten us confused.

Using this story as an example, what were the red flags I should have noticed? We never met, so I didn't know if he was the man in his pictures. Also, he said he was Swedish. I didn't know what a Swedish accent sounded like but his sounded more eastern European. When he tricked me into going to the Apple store and I thought he needed a manual, I should have been suspicious that he didn't tell me outright that he wanted me to buy actual computers for him.

It was a lesson learned. However, it did not deter me from trying to find one good man to share my love and life with. Then the Covid-19 pandemic started, making it even harder to find someone. I continued to use dating sites but was much more cautious. Some of the stories were so outrageous that they were funny, because these scammers did not stop trying to separate me from my money!

I had many different stories told to me by different men. One man romanced me, said he lived in my city and even sent me a dozen roses. Then he told me he had just received a letter from a storage company in Turkey. His father had left some things for him in a storage locker, and they were going to dispose of the contents unless picked up soon. So now my new friend said he was flying to Turkey. When he supposedly got there, he told me the contents amazed him. There were oil paintings, papers, and gold. When he eventually counted the gold, it added up to $96,000,000. Then he said he was told he couldn't transfer it home because he needed a license to transfer gold. But he tried anyway, then told me he was arrested for trying to transport the gold without a license. I didn't hear from him for three days, then he said he was being held at the airport and they hadn't fed him or allowed him to wash, so he was in a bad state. He was told he would be put in prison if he didn't pay $9,000, and asked me to email his lawyer friend. I did it just to see where the story was going. The lawyer said she contacted a friend of hers in Turkey who was a lawyer and had been to see my friend. He was in a bad state. The lawyer said they had amassed $4,500 for his bail but still needed the balance. I had already done a reverse phone number search and found a woman's name. This whole scam was being perpetrated by a woman in Florida. I did enjoy the roses though!

Another interesting story involved a "medical emergency." I briefly texted with a man in my city who said he had a doctor's appointment the next day and would call me after. Then I got a call from a "Dr. Lee," who said this man had lost a lot of blood in surgery. His blood type was rare and not stocked at the hospital. Then they sent me an address for a clinic that supposedly had the blood type and said it cost over $3,000. I didn't even know this man who supposedly needed blood!

Then there was a man with a strong Russian accent who said he worked for the UN in my city. He asked me out for a date that Friday. Late on Friday afternoon, he called to cancel our date. He said his boss was sending him on a triage mission to an island in the Atlantic called Machias Seal Island because there was a war between Canada and the U.S. I hadn't heard of a war between the U.S. and Canada, so I looked up the island. It is a slab of rock, totally inhospitable. The war is over sovereignty of fishing rights and the battles were being held in political circles and courtrooms. I texted him back, telling him that I knew he was a scammer.

One man texted me, told me his name and said he wanted to talk. He said he was from Switzerland, had moved his construction company to Canada and wanted to live there. I googled his name and found a company with his name, the same picture he was using on the dating site, and no mention of moving to Canada. He was a scammer and had used an existing company and the owner's picture before calling me to ask for money.

Another man said he lived in New York but was in Arizona, where his daughter was in boarding school. It was her birthday. He sent me pictures of an elaborate stage filled with fancifully wrapped gifts and pictures of the girl with her friends all dressed up for the big party. Then he told me she had a heart attack and was at the hospital having heart surgery. He told me he needed money to cover that surgery. I told him to sell the fancy gifts to pay for it and said that he should be ashamed of himself for using stolen pictures of a little girl.

Another man texted who said he lived nearby in Canada, but he always had an excuse when I would try to meet up. Despite his unwillingness to meet, he claimed to be interested in a relationship. He sent me lots of pictures of himself and his house. Then he said he had gotten hold of a few barrels of oil and had a buyer for them, but they were in the U.S. The transporter fees were more than he had on hand, so he asked if I could loan him $2,500. Of course, he said he would pay me back. I refused. Then he called me later to say he frequented a nearby restaurant. A waitress there had heard his story and had loaned him the money. He claimed that he had paid it back with interest. Sure he did!

Yet another man said he was working in Manitoba to build a bridge. He was a widower and looking for a relationship. I really liked him, and he pretended to really like me. He said he had an inspection by the people who hired him and was understandably anxious. After the inspection, he called to tell me that it didn't go well because an important part was broken. He had to order it from Germany, which would delay the project, and he would be in breach of contract. His decision was to go to Germany, hopefully to get the part sooner.

A few days later, he called to say that he had arrived in Germany but was now feeling sick and faint. He was in the hospital, and they were doing tests. Then he asked me if I would pay a bill for him that would have a penalty if it wasn't paid on time. He gave me the information and his banking numbers. I didn't see the harm since it wasn't my money he was using. The bill seemed to go through. Then he said he had another and asked if I would pay it for him using the same information. I tried it, and this time it wouldn't go through. A message came up that said fees of $19,000 were due and no further payments could be processed. Now I was suspicious, so I called the bank and asked about the fees. I was told the fees would only be around $300.

Now I knew I had been talking to a scammer. I swiped left, as these apps indicate you should do if you are not interested. He came back two months later, saying he loved me, and it was all a mix-up. After apologizing, he indicated that he was finally leaving Germany and was coming to my city to meet me. He gave me his credit card and asked me to book him a hotel. He said he wanted to buy a condo and asked me to get him some information. I thought, "What's the harm in that?" Then I got a picture of him lying in a hospital bed surrounded by doctors. He told me there had been an accident on the way to the airport and he was in bad shape. I told him I knew he was trying to scam me, and I wasn't interested in his games. Finally, he left me alone.

I later discovered some pictures of him on Google. He had four different names, and one picture of him was on a gay magazine cover kissing a man! These are but a few of the many lies I have been told by scammers. My hope is that by reading these examples, you start to see the pattern and can avoid the scams yourself.

Remember, if they make excuses and always have a reason why they can't ever meet up with you or even meet over a video chat, that should make you suspicious. Especially if they are claiming to live nearby.

Here are many of the popular stories being used by scammers:

They work on an oil rig, and they don't have access to their money. So, they need yours. Of course, they will pay you back. I found that any story about working in oil, like being a contractor in charge of a project involving oil, is suspect.

One man, who I was suspicious of, told me he was in charge of an oil project in Dubai. I checked out the pictures of him at the top or on an oil rig, and a picture revealing much more than I ever wanted to see. I searched his pictures and he had transposed his face onto the face of an actual person. Awful!

You may hear a story of a gemologist who is working in a mine somewhere like Papua, New Guinea and being attacked by natives because the workers are desecrating their land. Then he will tell you he is ready to come home and needs money to import the gems. He will ask you for it, and of course he will pay you back.

These men have romanced you, thinking that you are convinced that what they are saying is the truth. Then they bring up a sick relative who needs an operation and they need you to pay for it.

I spoke to a man who said he was an orthopedic surgeon working with the U.S. Army in Yemen. I googled "orthopedic surgeon working with the U.S. Army in Yemen," and a warning came up that this was a scam. For scammers targeting the U.S., using pictures of military members, including admirals and army commanders, is a common way to gain sympathy and get people to part with their money.

Turkey has been a very popular location that scammers have used because it is a place that many are not familiar with. The customs and laws might be different and so they feel you are more likely to accept the reasons why they need money. One of the most popular stories is bidding on a project, winning the bid, and then heading off to Turkey, where they then tell you one of the following:

- They have been robbed and need your money to help them out.

- They are hiring workers and found that they didn't expect them to be so expensive, and they need your money.

- They have ordered equipment and didn't calculate the high import fees and duty.

- They need tech equipment and can't get any in English over there, and want you to buy some and ship to them.

Another story is they are military working abroad, usually as doctors, particularly orthopedic surgeons. They befriend you and say they want to come to you to meet, but in order to leave their unit, you will have to fill out a form saying you are a girlfriend or a fiancé and will guarantee their safety. It costs a few thousand dollars which they will ask you to send them.

Clearly, these stories are meant to prey on your goodwill and emotions, keeping you from questioning their stories. Now that you have seen a sampling of the types of stories they use, let's talk about some practical ways to protect yourself from these scammers.

Protect Yourself from Scammers

The first way to protect yourself is to never give your money to someone you don't know or have never met! Remember, their goal is to part you from your hard-earned money, and any story they create is designed to get you to give them money without question.

The second way is to look out for red flags that indicate a scammer. Here are a few of them:

- Watch for poor spelling and sentence structure.

- They may want you to go onto Hangouts where it is more private, and where they can't be easily detected.

- They will tell you they are widowed, that their wife died in a horrible accident or from cancer. Their child is in boarding school in England or has a nanny.

- If divorced, their wife cheated on them or was a drug addict and a danger to their child.

- The picture of the attractive person you think you are talking to is not real. The photo has been stolen. Look carefully around the face and see if you see any shadows or crooked parts. They sometimes copy a face over another and paste it on.

- They usually have two first names.

- They will ask if you have a house or a car, and what you do for a living, to see if you are worth their time to scam you.

- They will try to get as much information from you as they can, like birthdates, kids' names, etc., to try to figure out your passwords.

- They will say they will come and see you, but they NEVER WILL! And they will have a million excuses why not.

- They have been in an accident, they were robbed, been detained, need a new phone, their passport was stolen, their contract won't allow them to leave or do a video chat, their child is sick, their sister needs an operation, etc.

- They will have a heavy accent. They will tell you they are mixed and raised in the U.S. Italian, Polish, and other European are very popular. But they definitely don't sound North American.

- If asked to send inappropriate photos, never send them. They could be used as blackmail against you later to get more money.

- Once you send money, it can be considered money laundering and you could be in trouble with the law!

Here are some points to keep in mind about images. Many of them are stolen and their photoshopping is not great. Look closely and don't take an image at face value. Also, use some of these tools to help you determine the origin of an image.

Go to Google and enter Yandex images. The site is Russian, but you can still see photos. Take a snapshot of your suspect and enter it on the site. It may show you that he is on the site where you found him. Scroll through the images and see if you find that picture or one that looks like him. Sometimes he will give you a name that isn't his. Many celebrities' pictures are used. You can also use Facebook to search the image, which can help you see that it is fake.

Many of them will ask you for iTunes or pre-paid cards that they can trade for money. This system is meant to get past your guard, but achieves the same objective, which is cash for them.

Many of the scammers don't start out asking for a large amount. They will ask you for a little at first, and then the next time it will be more, and so on. Their focus is on getting as much out of you as they can. As they build up to bigger amounts, they are counting on you being too heavily invested to stop sending them money.

I believe that it is possible to meet someone using these sites, but I also know that you have to follow the method of trust but verify. Here are a few ways to do just that:

- Get them to phone you, or ask for their phone number. Use a Reverse Lookup site to check out the number and see if it's where they say they live.

- Listen carefully to the voice. See if you can figure out where their accent is from. An African man's voice is very distinctive. They also have a high-pitched girlish laugh. The point is that the voice is not likely to match up with who they claim to be.

- Their favorite meal tends to be chicken and rice, which is very popular in Africa. If they write very lengthy messages about themselves and how they are looking for love, and sound so nice, it's probably copied and pasted from information that's been passed around.

- Don't be fooled by fake documents, like a plane ticket or bank statement. They can make very good copies of these documents. However, you can look up these companies and see if they are legitimate. Many times, they are not.

I hope my story and what I have learned will give you the courage to reveal your own experience to others. If they ask you how you could be so stupid as to give away your money to a scammer, tell them to read my book so they can understand how easy it is easy to fall into their trap with tales of love.

At the same time, I hope that by sharing these tips and tools, you can avoid being caught by these scammers.

The more we talk about it, the more it will be understood, the more people will know what to avoid, and we will expose these criminals. It may be embarrassing for the victim but the best way to stop it is to expose it. I also want to note here that these scammers are willing to try new stories, but the mode of operation never really changes. If they know you have sent money once, they will be persistent in trying to get you to do it again. Be willing to stand up for yourself!

The FBI is now warning people to beware of romance scammers looking for more than love. Millions have been stolen by these criminals. The consequences of these scams are financially and emotionally devastating to victims. Very few of the victims ever get their money back. Others may never recover from their heartbreak and financial loss.

Don't be ashamed if you have been a victim. You are not alone. If you know someone who has been a victim, be kind. Share this information to help others avoid being a victim. We need to help each other to avoid these predators!

The Woman of my Dreams and a Million Dollars

RAYMOND AARON, ORBIT™ Coach

I teach a rather unique spiritual workshop with the most unusual name, The Mulberry Hill Gang™ (MHG). The promise is that you get whatever you wish. It's a giant promise and I truly deliver on that promise.

I had been alone and lonely for a decade. I wanted a woman in my life, but found no one. My friend Wendy recommended I teach my amazing MHG once again and instead of being just the teacher, I should be the teacher and a student. She further explained that if I were also a student, I could postulate the woman of my dreams just showing up. I was so excited that I added a second postulate that I would earn $1 million faster than anyone on earth had ever earned a million dollars.

My step-daughters imposed a rule on me that I could not date anyone younger than them. That seems reasonable.

My business partner Geoff, an accountant, imposed yet another rule on me: that I could not date revenue or expenses. What? What does that even mean? He explained that revenue was clients and expenses meant staff. I accepted.

The first day of my miracle workshop MHG arrived ... and there she was in the front row. Young. Beautiful. Sexy. Stunningly-dressed. Brilliant answers to my questions. She laughed at my jokes. She asked insightful questions. I was smitten.

But I needed to know her age because of my commitment to my stepdaughters. I asked every participant to submit their birthday with year. I discarded all others and looked only at hers. She was just months older than my older stepdaughter. Phew.

But what was worse is that she was for sure a client. I checked our company database and she wasn't in it. But she was definitely in a paid course. So, I strolled up to her at a break to ask why she wasn't in our database. She said she had not paid for the course, rather her boss had paid for it and was called away to China on short notice to inspect a factory. He had forgotten what the course was about but gave her the ticket to attend. So, impossibly, she was attending a paid course ... but she hadn't paid. Hence, she was not a client. And, she was old enough.

On our first date, it got even weirder. I look much younger than my actual age, so I confessed to her my age. I could see she was subtracting her age from my age and she said 17. She made an unhappy look on her face meaning that that was the very very outside limit of what she could accept. However, you made a subtraction error. I'm 27 years older. But, I wanted to be her lover, not her math tutor, so I said nothing. Fortunately, she fell in love with me before she discovered her subtraction error.

And that's how the Spiritual Universe removed all obstacles to allow me to find the woman of my dreams on the very first day of MHG.

And, as an enticing footnote, you will recall that I added that I wanted to earn one million dollars faster than anyone on earth had ever earned that amount of money. Shortly after that offering of MHG, a promoter called me to ask if I would like to present at a giant summit to be attended by 17,000 eager entrepreneurs. The promoter gave me the very best speaker slot, every seat was filled, and I earned over one million dollars in that speech. That was by far the most I'd ever earned and since that date I have never earned anywhere near that amount since. Just once. Just from that startling postulate!

Please connect with Raymond Aaron at help@aaron.com to be considered to attend the powerful spiritual workshop: Mulberry Hill Gang.

Happiness: How to Experience the "Real Deals"

MARCI SHIMOFF

I was 41 years old, stretched out on a lounge chair by my pool and reflecting on my life. I had achieved all that I thought I needed to be happy.

You see, when I was a child, I thought there would be five main things that would ensure that I'd be happy: a successful career helping people, a loving husband, a comfortable home, a great body, and a wonderful circle of friends. After years of study, hard work, and a few "lucky breaks," I finally had them all. (Okay, so my body didn't quite look like Halle Berry's—but four out of five isn't bad!) You think I'd have been on the top of the world.

But surprisingly I wasn't. I felt an emptiness inside that the outer successes of life couldn't fill. I was also afraid that if I lost any of those things, I might be miserable. Sadly, I knew I wasn't alone in feeling this way.

While happiness is the one thing we all truly want, so few people really experience the deep and lasting fulfillment that fills our soul. Why aren't we finding it?

Because, in the words of the old country western song, we're looking for happiness in "all the wrong places."

Looking around, I saw that the happiest people I knew weren't the most successful and famous. Some were married, some were single. Some had lots of money, and some didn't have a dime. Some of them even had health challenges. From where I stood, there seemed to be no rhyme or reason to what made people happy. The obvious question became: *Could a person actually be happy for no reason?*

I had to find out.

So I threw myself into the study of happiness. I interviewed scores of scientists, as well as 100 unconditionally happy people. (I call them the Happy 100.) I delved into the research from the burgeoning field of positive psychology, the study of the positive traits that enable people to enjoy meaningful, fulfilling, and happy lives.

What I found changed my life. To share this knowledge with others, I wrote a book called *Happy for No Reason: 7 Steps to Being Happy from the Inside Out*.

One day, as I sat down to compile my findings, all the pieces of the puzzle fell into place. I had a simple, but profound "a-ha"—there's a continuum of happiness.

Unhappy: We all know what this means: life seems flat. Some of the signs are anxiety, fatigue, feeling blue or low—your "garden-variety" unhappiness. This isn't the same as clinical depression, which is characterized by deep despair and hopelessness that dramatically interferes with your ability to live a normal life, and for which professional help is absolutely necessary.

Happy for Bad Reason: When people are unhappy, they often try to make themselves feel better by indulging in addictions or behaviors that may feel good in the moment but are ultimately detrimental. They seek the highs that come from drugs, alcohol, excessive sex, "retail therapy," compulsive gambling, over-eating, and too much television-watching, to name a few. This kind of "happiness" is hardly happiness at all. It is only a temporary way to numb or escape our unhappiness through fleeting experiences of pleasure.

Happy for Good Reason: This is what people usually mean by happiness: having good relationships with our family and friends, success in our careers, financial security, a nice house or car, or using our talents and strengths well. It's the pleasure we derive from having the healthy things in our lives that we want.

Don't get me wrong. I'm all for this kind of happiness! It's just that it's only half the story. Being Happy for Good Reason depends on the external conditions of our lives—if these conditions change or are lost, our happiness usually goes too. Relying solely on this type of happiness is where a lot of our fear is stemming from these days. We're afraid the things we think we need to be happy may be slipping from our grasp.

Deep inside, I think we all know that life isn't meant to be about getting by, numbing our pain, or having everything "under control." True happiness doesn't come from merely collecting an assortment of happy experiences. At our core, we know there's something more than this.

There is. It's the next level on the happiness continuum—Happy for No Reason.

Happy for No Reason: This is true happiness—a state of peace and well-being that isn't dependent on external circumstances.

Happy for No Reason isn't elation, euphoria, mood spikes, or peak experiences that don't last. It doesn't mean grinning like a fool 24/7 or experiencing a superficial high. Happy for No Reason isn't an emotion. In fact, when you are Happy for No Reason, you can have *any* emotion—including sadness, fear, anger, or hurt—but you still experience that underlying state of peace and well-being.

When you're Happy for No Reason, you *bring* happiness to your outer experiences rather than trying to *extract* happiness from them. You don't need to manipulate the world around you to try to make yourself happy. You live *from* happiness, rather than *for* happiness.

This is a revolutionary concept. Most of us focus on being Happy for Good Reason, stringing together as many happy experiences as we can, like beads in a necklace, to create a happy life. We have to spend a lot of time and energy trying to find just the right beads so we can have a "happy necklace."

Being Happy for No Reason, in our necklace analogy, is like having a happy string. No matter what beads we put on our necklace—good, bad, or indifferent—our inner experience, which is the string that runs through them all, is happy, and creates a happy life.

Happy for No Reason is a state that's been spoken of in virtually all spiritual and religious traditions throughout history. The concept is universal. In Buddhism, it is called causeless joy; in Christianity, the kingdom of Heaven within; and in Judaism it is called *ashrei*, an inner sense of holiness and health. In Islam it is called *falah*, happiness and well-being; and in Hinduism it is called *ananda*, or pure bliss. Some traditions refer to it as an enlightened or awakened state.

So how can you be Happy for No Reason?

Science is verifying the way. Researchers in the field of positive psychology have found that we each have a "happiness set-point," that determines our level of happiness. No matter what happens, whether it's something as exhilarating as winning the lottery or as challenging as a horrible accident, most people eventually return to their original happiness level. Like your weight set-point, which keeps the scale hovering around the same number, your happiness set-point will remain the same **unless you make a concerted effort to change it.** In the same way you'd crank up the thermostat to get comfortable on a chilly day, you actually have the power to reprogram your happiness set-point to a higher level of peace and well-being. The secret lies in practicing the habits of happiness.

Some books and programs will tell you that you can simply decide to be happy. They say just make up your mind to be happy—and you will be.

I don't agree.

You can't just decide to be happy, any more than you can decide to be fit or to be a great piano virtuoso and expect instant mastery. You can, however, decide to take the necessary steps, like exercising or taking piano lessons—and by practicing those skills, you can get in shape or give recitals. In the same way, you can become Happy for No Reason through practicing the habits of happy people.

All of your habitual thoughts and behaviors in the past have created specific neural pathways in the wiring in your brain, like grooves in a record. When we think or behave a certain way over and over, the neural pathway is strengthened and the groove becomes deeper—the way a well-traveled route through a field eventually becomes a clear-cut path. Unhappy people tend to have more negative neural pathways. This is why you can't just ignore the realities of your brain's wiring and *decide* to be happy! To raise your level of happiness, you have to create new grooves.

Scientists used to think that once a person reached adulthood, the brain was fairly well "set in stone" and there wasn't much you could do to change it. But new research is revealing exciting information about the brain's neuroplasticity: when you think, feel, and act in different ways, the brain changes and actually rewires itself. You aren't doomed to the same negative neural pathways for your whole life. Leading brain researcher Dr. Richard Davidson, of the University of Wisconsin says, "Based on what we know of the plasticity of the brain, we can think of things like happiness and compassion as skills that are no different from learning to play a musical instrument or tennis ... it is possible to train our brains to be happy."

While a few of the Happy 100 I interviewed were born happy, most of them learned to be happy by practicing habits that supported their happiness. That means wherever you are on the happiness continuum, it's entirely in your power to raise your happiness level.

In the course of my research, I uncovered 21 core happiness habits that anyone can use to become happier and stay that way. You can find all 21 happiness habits at www.HappyForNoReason.com.

Here are a few tips to get you started:

1. **Incline your mind toward joy.** Have you noticed that your mind tends to register the negative events in your life more than the positive? If you get 10 compliments in a day and one criticism, what do you remember? For most people, it's the criticism. Scientists call this our "negativity bias"—our primitive survival wiring that causes us to pay more attention to the negative than the positive. To reverse this bias, get into the daily habit of consciously registering the positive around you: the sun on your skin, the taste of a favorite food, a smile or kind word from a co-worker or friend. Once you notice something positive, take a moment to savor it deeply and feel it; make it more than just a mental observation. Spend 20 seconds soaking up the happiness you feel.

2. **Let love lead.** One way to power up your heart's flow is by sending loving kindness to your friends and family, as well as strangers you pass on the street. Next time you're waiting for the elevator at work, stuck in a line at the store or caught up in traffic, send a silent wish to the people you see for their happiness, well-being, and health. Simply wishing others well switches on the "pump" in your own heart that generates love and creates a strong current of happiness.

3. **Lighten your load.** To make a habit of letting go of worries and negative thoughts, start by letting go on the physical level. Cultural anthropologist Angeles Arrien recommends giving or throwing away 27 items a day for nine days. This deceptively simple practice will help you break attachments that no longer serve you.

4. **Make your cells happy.** Your brain contains a veritable pharmacopeia of natural happiness-enhancing neurochemicals—endorphins, serotonin, oxytocin, and dopamine—just waiting to be released to every organ and cell in your body. The way that you eat, move, rest, and even your facial expression can shift the balance of your body's feel-good-chemicals, or "Joy Juice," in your favor. To dispense some extra Joy Juice—smile. Scientists have discovered that smiling decreases stress hormones and boosts happiness chemicals, which increase the body's T-cells, reduce pain, and enhance relaxation. You may not feel like it, but smiling—even artificially to begin with—starts the ball rolling and will turn into a real smile in short order.

5. **Hang with the happy.** We catch the emotions of those around us just like we catch their colds—it's called emotional contagion. So it's important to make wise choices about the company you keep. Create appropriate boundaries with emotional bullies and "happiness vampires" who suck the life out of you. Develop your happiness "dream team"—a mastermind or support group you meet with regularly to keep you steady on the path of raising your happiness.

"Happily ever after" isn't just for fairytales or for only the lucky few. Imagine experiencing inner peace and well-being as the backdrop for everything else in your life. When you're Happy for No Reason, it's not that your life always looks perfect—it's that, however it looks, you'll still be happy!

Sex, Love and Relationships

DR. JOHN GRAY

Just as great sex is important to lasting love, good health is important to sex and relationships. About 12 years ago, I cured myself of early stage Parkinson's disease. The doctors were amazed, but my wife was even more amazed. She noted that our relationship and sex life had become dramatically better. It turns out that the natural supplements I used to reverse Parkinson's can also make you more attentive and loving in your relationship. At that point, I realized that good relationship skills alone were not enough to sustain love and passion for a lifetime.

I shared many insights gained from my 40 years' experience as a marriage counselor and coach in *Men Are From Mars, Women Are From Venus*. And while my insights go a long way towards helping men and women understand and support each other, good communication skills alone are not always enough. For better relationships, we not only need to be healthy, but we must also experience optimum brain function.

If you are tired, depressed, anxious, not sleeping well, or in pain, then certainly romantic feelings will become a thing of the past. My recovery from Parkinson's revealed to me the profound connection between the quality of our health and our relationships. This insight has motivated me, over the past twelve years, to research the secrets of optimum health as a foundation for lasting love.

These are health secrets that are generally not explored in medical school. In medical school, doctors are indoctrinated into the culture of examining the symptoms, identifying the sickness, and prescribing a drug to treat that sickness. They learn very little about how to be healthy or to sustain successful relationships.

There are no university courses entitled "Better Nutrition For Better Sex". Drugs sometimes save lives, but they also have negative side effects that do little to preserve the passion in a relationship. Ideally, drugs should be used as a last resort and 90 % of our health plan should be drug free. From this perspective, the heath care crisis, as well as our high rate of divorce in America, is indirectly caused by our dependence on doctors and prescription drugs.

Most people have not even considered that taking prescribed drugs (even for the small stuff) can weaken their relationships, which in turn makes them more vulnerable to more disease. For example, if you are feeling depressed or anxious, a drug may numb your pain, but it does nothing to help you correct the cause of your problem. It can even prevent you from feeling your natural motivation to get the emotional support you need. In a variety of ways, our common health complaints are all expressions of two major conditions: our lack of education to identify and support unmet gender-specific emotional needs; and our lack of education to identify and support unmet gender-specific nutritional needs.

With an understanding of natural solutions that have been around for thousands of years, drugs are not needed to treat many common complaints. Some symptoms like low energy, weight gain, allergies, hormonal imbalance, mood swings, poor sleep, indigestion, lack of focus, ADD and ADHD, procrastination, low motivation, memory loss, decreased libido, PMS, vaginal dryness, muscle and joint pain, or the lack of passion in life and/or our relationships can be treated drug-free. By using drugs (even over-the-counter drugs) to treat these common complaints, our bodies and relationships are weakened, making us more vulnerable to bigger and more costly health challenges like cancer, diabetes, heart disease, auto-immune disease, dementia, and Alzheimer's. In simple terms, by handling the easy stuff (the common complaints) without doctors and drugs, we can protect ourselves from the big stuff (cancer, heart disease, dementia, etc.) We can be healthy and also enjoy lasting love and passion in our personal lives.

Even if you are taking anti-depressants or hormone replacement therapy, sometimes all it takes to stop treating the symptom is to directly handle the cause. With specific mineral orotates (something most people have never heard of) or omega three oil from the brains of salmon, your stress levels immediately drop and you begin to feel happy and in love again.

For every health challenge, we have explored the effects on our relationships, with as well as natural remedies that can sometimes produce immediate positive results. You can find these natural solutions to common health complaints for free at my website: www.MarsVenus.com.

What they don't teach in medical school is how to be healthy and happy without the use of drugs or hormone replacement. By refusing drugs and taking responsibility for your health, a wealth of new possibilities can become available to you. We are designed to be healthy and happy, and it is within our reach if we commit to increasing our knowledge.

New research regarding the brain differences in men and women reveals how specific nutritional supplements, combined with gender-specific relationship and self-nurturing skills, can stimulate the hormones of health, happiness and increased energy. Over the past 10 years in my healing center in California, I witnessed how natural solutions coupled with gender-specific relationship skills could solve our common health complaints without drugs. By addressing these common complaints without prescribed drugs, not only do we feel better, but our relationships have the potential to improve dramatically.

Ultimately the cause of all our common complaints is higher stress levels. Researchers around the world all agree that chronic stress levels in our bodies provide a basis for any and all disease to take hold. An easy and quick solution for lowering our stress reactions is specific nutritional support combined with gender-smart relationship skills. Extra nutritional support is needed because stress depletes the body very quickly of essential nutrients. When a car engine is running more quickly, it uses fuel more quickly. When we are stressed, we need both extra nutrients and extra emotional support. Understanding what we need to take and where to get it requires education. Every week day at www.MarsVenus.com I have a live daily show where I freely answer questions and provide this much-needed new gender-specific insight.

At www.MarsVenus.com, we are happy to share what we have learned for creating healthy bodies and positive relationships. You can find a host of natural solutions for common complaints and feel confident that you have the power to feel fully alive with an abundance of energy and positive feelings that will enrich all your relationships.

Unleashing Your Full Potential

BRIAN TRACY

One of the qualities of "Authorities," of superior men and women, is that they are extremely self-reliant. They accept complete responsibility for themselves and everything that happens to them. They look to themselves as the source of their successes, and as the main cause of their problems and difficulties. High achievers say, "If it's to be, it's up to me." When things aren't moving along as fast as they want, they ask themselves, "What is it in me that is causing this problem?" They refuse to make excuses or to blame people. Instead, they look for ways to overcome obstacles and to make progress.

Totally self-responsible people look upon themselves as self-employed. They see themselves as the presidents of their own personal services corporations. They realize that no matter who signs their paycheck, in the final analysis, they work for themselves. Because they have this attitude of self-employment, they take a strategic approach to their work.

The essential element in strategic planning for a corporation or a business entity is the concept of "return on equity." All business planning is aimed at organizing and reorganizing the resources of the business in such a way as to increase the financial returns to the business owners. It is to increase the quantity of output relative to the quantity of input. It is to focus on areas of high profitability and return and simultaneously, to withdraw resources from areas of low profitability and low return. Companies that do this effectively in a rapidly changing environment are the ones that survive and prosper. Companies that fail to do this form of strategic analysis are those that fall behind and often disappear.

INCREASE YOUR RETURN ON ENERGY

To achieve everything you are capable of achieving as a person, you also must become a skilled strategic planner with regard to your life and work. But instead of aiming to increase your return on equity, your goal is to increase your return on energy.

Most people in our society start off in life with little more than their ability to work. More than 80 percent of the millionaires in North America started with little or nothing. Most people have been broke, or nearly broke, several times during their young-adult years. But the ones who eventually get ahead are those who do certain things in certain ways, over and over. These actions set them apart from the masses.

Perhaps the most important thing they do, consciously or unconsciously, is to look at themselves strategically, thinking about how they can better use themselves in the marketplace, how they can best capitalize on their strengths and abilities to increase their financial returns to themselves and their families.

INCREASE YOUR EARNING ABILITY

Your most valuable financial asset is your earning ability, your ability to earn money. Properly applied to the marketplace, it's like a pump. By exploiting your earning ability, you can pump tens of thousands of extra dollars a year into your pocket. All your knowledge, education, skills and experience contribute toward your earning ability, your ability to get results for which someone will pay you good money.

Your earning ability is like farmland. If you don't take excellent care of it, if you don't fertilize it and cultivate it and water it on a regular basis, it soon loses its ability to produce the kind of harvest that you desire. Successful men and women are those who are extremely aware of the importance and value of their earning ability, and they work every day to keep it growing and current with the demands of the marketplace.

One of your greatest responsibilities in life is to identify, develop and maintain an important marketable skill. It is to become very good at doing something for which there is a strong market demand.

DEVELOP A COMPETITIVE ADVANTAGE

In corporate strategy, we call this the development of a "competitive advantage." For a company, a competitive advantage is defined as an area of excellence in producing a product or service that gives the company a distinct edge over its competition.

In capitalizing on your strengths, as the president of your own personal services corporation, you also must have a clear competitive advantage. You also must have an area of excellence. You must do something that makes you different from and better than your competitors.

Your ability to identify and develop this competitive advantage is the most important thing you do in the world of work. It's the key to maintaining your earning ability. It's the foundation of your financial success. Without it, you're simply a pawn in a rapidly changing environment. But with a distinct competitive advantage, based on your strengths and abilities, you can write your own ticket. You can take charge of your own life. You can always get a job. And the more distinct your competitive advantage, the more money you can earn and the more places in which you can earn it.

FOUR KEYS TO COMPETITIVE ADVANTAGE

There are four keys to the strategic marketing of yourself and your services. These are applicable to huge companies such as General Motors, to candidates running for election, and to individuals who want to accomplish the very most in the very shortest period of time.

The first of these four keys is specialization. No one can be all things to all people. A "jack-of-all-trades" is also a "master of none." That career path usually leads to a dead end. Specialization is the key. Men and women who are successful have a series of general skills, but they also have one or two areas where they have developed the ability to perform in an outstanding manner.

Your decision about how, where, when and why you are going to specialize in a particular area of endeavor is perhaps the most important decision you will ever make in your career. It was well said that if you don't think about the future, you can't have one. The major reason why so many people are finding their jobs eliminated, and finding themselves unemployed for long periods of time, is because they didn't look down the road of life far enough and prepare themselves well enough for the time when their current jobs would expire. They suddenly found themselves out of gas on a lonely road, facing a long walk back to regular and well-paying employment. Don't let this happen to you.

In determining your area of specialization, put your current job aside for the moment, and take the time to look deeply into yourself. Analyze yourself from every point of view. Rise above yourself, and look at your lifetime of activities and accomplishments in determining what your area of specialization could be or should be.

You might be doing exactly the right job for you at this moment. You might already be capitalizing on all your strengths, and your current work might be ideally suited to your likes and dislikes, to your temperament and your personality. Nevertheless, you owe it to yourself to be continually expanding the scope of your vision and looking toward the future to see where you might want to be going in the months and years ahead. Remember, the best way to predict the future is to create it.

You possess special talents and abilities that make you unique, different from anyone else who has ever lived. The odds of there being another person just like you are more than 50 billion to one. Your remarkable and unusual combination of education, experience, knowledge, problems, successes, difficulties and challenges, and your way of looking at and reacting to life, make you extraordinary. You have within you potential competencies and attributes that can enable you to accomplish virtually anything you want in life. Even if you lived for another 100 years, it would not be enough time for you to plumb the depths of your potential. You will never be able to use more than a small part of your inborn abilities. Your main job is to decide which of your talents you're going to exploit and develop to their highest and best possible use right now.

YOUR AREA OF EXCELLENCE

What is your area of excellence? What are you especially good at doing right now? If things continue as they are, what are you likely to be good at in the future—one or two or even five years from today? Is this a marketable skill with a growing demand, or is your field changing in such a way that you are going to have to change as well if you want to keep up with it? Looking into the future, what could be your area of excellence if you were to go to work on yourself and your abilities? What should be your area of excellence if you want to rise to the top of your field, make an excellent living and take complete control of your financial future?

When I was 22, I answered an advertisement for a copywriter for an advertising agency. As it happened, I had failed high-school English, and I really had no idea what a copywriter did. I remember the executive who interviewed me and how nice he was at pointing out that I wasn't at all qualified for the job.

But something happened to me in the course of the interview process. The more I thought about it, the more I thought how much I would like to write advertising. Having been turned down flat during my first interview, I decided to learn more about the field.

I went to the city library and began to check out and read books on advertising and copywriting. Over the next six months, while I worked as a clerk in a department store, I spent many hours devouring them. At the same time, I applied for copywriting jobs to advertising agencies in the city. I started with the smaller agencies first. When they turned me down, I asked them why? What was wrong with my application? What did I need to learn more about? What books would they recommend? And to this day, I remember that virtually everyone I spoke with was helpful to me.

By the end of six months, I had read every book on advertising and copywriting in the city library, and I had applied to every agency in the city, working up from the smallest agency to the very largest in the country. And by the time I had reached that level, I was ready. I was offered jobs as a junior copywriter by both the number-one and number-two agencies in the country. I took the job with the number-one agency and was very successful in a short period of time.

THERE ARE NO LIMITS

The point of this story is that you can become almost anything you need to become, in order to accomplish almost anything you want to accomplish, if you simply decide what it is and then learn what you need to learn. This is such an obvious fact that most people miss it completely.

Some years later, I heard that one could earn a lot of money in real estate development. Again, I went to the library and began checking out and reading all the books I could find on real estate development. At the time, I had no money, no contacts and no knowledge of the industry. But I knew the great secret: I could learn what I needed to learn so that I could do what I wanted to do.

Within 12 months, I had tied up a piece of property with a $100 deposit and a 30-day option. I put together a proposal for a shopping center. I tentatively arranged for two major anchor tenants and several minor tenants that together took up 85 percent of the square footage I had proposed. Then I sold 75 percent of the entire package to a major development company in exchange for the company's putting up all the cash and providing me with the resources and people I needed to manage the construction of the shopping center and the completion of the leasing. Virtually everything that I did I had learned from books written by real estate experts, books on the shelves of the local library.

As you might have noticed, the fields of advertising and copywriting and real estate development are very different. But these experiences, and every business situation I have been in over the years, had one element in common. Success in each area was based on the decision, first, to specialize in that area and, second, to become extremely knowledgeable in that area so that I could do a good job.

In looking at your current and past experiences for an area of specialization, one of the most important questions to ask yourself is, "What activities have been most responsible for my success in life to date?"

How did you get from where you were to where you are today? What talents and abilities seem to come easily to you? What things do you do well that seem to be difficult for most other people? What things do you most enjoy doing? What things do you find most intrinsically motivating? What activities make you happy when you are doing them?

In capitalizing on your strengths, your level of interest, excitement and enthusiasm about the particular job or activity is a key factor. You'll always do best and make the most money in a field that you really enjoy. It will be an area that you like to think about and talk about and read about and learn about. Successful people love what they do, and they can hardly wait to get to it each day. Doing their work makes them happy, and the happier they are, the more enthusiastically they do it, and the better they do it as well.

DIFFERENTIATION IS THE KEY TO SUCCESS IN BUSINESS

In capitalizing on your strengths, the second key to success is differentiation. You must decide what you're going to do to be not only different at doing but also better than your competitors in the field. Remember, you have to be good in only one specific area to move ahead of the pack. And you must decide what that area should be.

SEGMENT YOUR MARKET

The third strategic principle in capitalizing on your strengths is segmentation. You have to look at the marketplace and determine where you can best apply yourself, with your unique talents and abilities, to give yourself the highest possible return on energy expended. What customers, companies, or markets, can best utilize your special talents and offer you the most in terms of financial rewards and future opportunities?

FOCUS AND CONCENTRATION

The final key to personal strategic planning is concentration. Once you have decided the area in which you are going to specialize, how you are going to differentiate yourself, and where in the marketplace you can best apply your strengths, your final job is to concentrate all of your energy on becoming excellent in that specific area. The marketplace only pays extraordinary rewards for extraordinary performance.

In the final analysis, everything that you have done up to now is simply the groundwork for becoming outstanding in your chosen field. When you become very good at doing what people want and need, and are willing to pay for, you begin moving rapidly into the top ranks of the highest paid people everywhere.

And there are no limits.

Exceeding Expectations While Building Long-Term Relationships

ALICE MADISHA & JANNIE SMITH

"I offer my expertise and experience for hire in order to help a group of people reach the summit."

-Anatoli Boukreev

Imagine the hustle and bustle of a shopping centres and warehouses that employ hundreds of people and where thousands of people come to shop every single week. Imagine those shopping centres and office parks needing new shop fronts, tiling and mall ceilings. To some people, that sounds like a logistical nightmare, but to Smith and Madisha Construction, that was just another day at work.

Extraordinary problems call for extraordinary solutions, and we're the problem solvers who can take away the stress and the chaos that you might have been worried about. Whether you are a large business owner, a project manager or a contractor, we step in to make sure that the job gets done on time, safely and under the budget that you designate. We don't believe in excuses; at the end of the day, all we believe in is getting the job done.

GETTING THE JOB DONE RIGHT OUR WAY

The Boskruin Centre, owned by Eris Properties, is a busy shopping centre that serves the commercial needs of a demanding urban community, and we knew going in that no one wanted to see any loss of revenue. When we hit the scene, we could immediately see how important it was for Eris Properties, the owners of the Boskruin Shopping Centre, that everything stays operational.

Other companies would have recommended shutting portions of the centre down as the crews went to work, but the more we looked at the situation, the less we wanted to do that. Eris Properties wanted the job done as quickly and as painlessly as possible, but we realized that that could absolutely happen with zero lost of income to our clients and to the shops at the mall.

Working in close with our client, an amazing architectural firm and an excellent electrical engineering crew, we studied the situation and made the decision to work mostly at night. This allowed our client's requirements to be met, it allowed all of our client's tenants to keep on doing business as usual, and we made sure that the shopping centre's customers didn't go away empty-handed because of construction.

The end result was a shopping centre that shone like new, with fresh façades, ceilings and even a brand new parking deck. Today, we continue to work with Eris Properties, streamlining their projects and satisfying their need for timely delivery of immaculate and high-quality work.

MAKING THE MOVING PIECES WORK

Whenever you undertake a major project, there is a risk. For many of our clients, construction is something that happens once in a great while. For some of them, it is the birth of a dream. While they have the drive and the dream, we're the ones who bring our expertise regarding the construction process to the table.

Here's what you might not know about construction projects. They are not one large entity moving steadily towards completion. If they were, no one would ever scream about budget issues, unforeseen problems, safety issues and more!

Instead, a construction project is a lot more like a clock. There are a dozen small pieces all working together to get towards one final goal, and when a single component becomes misaligned, goes missing or is otherwise out of order, you are looking at a full stop!

If your construction project is the watch, we're the watchmakers. We go in and make sure that every single part of the project is operating the way that it should. We understand that unless everything works together perfectly, your project grinds to a halt. In a worst case scenario, it comes crashing down.

Don't think that it can't happen to you. With our long experience in the industry, we've seen it happen, and it's not pretty!

For an example that any project at all can relate to, let's talk about safety. Accidents on a construction site can lead to tragedy, and at the very least, they can lead to fines and even shut-downs. When the Department of Labour steps in, it can take weeks or even months before they rule that your site is safe to resume work. Occupational Safety and Health Act (OSHACT) regulations are strict and exacting, and unfortunately, many of the emerging contractors that you are working with might be unfamiliar with them.

As they say so often, ignorance of the law is no excuse, and when the Department of Labour decides that your site is unsafe, you are looking at a serious hurdle to your project's safety. We've seen projects get cancelled over safety issues, and that is where we step in.

SAFETY FIRST

As safety consultants, we ensure that every single one of your contractors know how to run the site in accordance with every single OHSACT requirement. We make sure that everyone is up to date on Risk Assessments, the correct safe working procedurals and more. A construction site can be a dangerous place, and though the OHSACT requirements make them safer, they are not necessarily intuitive.

If it sounds like the safety requirements for a construction project can actually wrap your project up in red tape and an endless round of paperwork, fees and halts, that's because they can! This is the kind of issue that can send your project grinding to a halt with no restart date in sight. Safety is big business, and if you don't know how to play the game, you're going to find yourself sitting on the sidelines with nothing getting done.

In our role as your safety consultants, we make sure that your people get the training that they need with regards to both the paperwork side of things as well as the essential on-site safety training. More than just giving them a check-list of what to do, we get in there and we show them how to run site safety meetings and how to make sure that the sub-contractors chosen are trained for the job.

By the end of our involvement in the safety segment of your project, every single person involved in your project will have the certificates necessary to work from the correct certification agencies. We do all of this in a timely fashion and on the budget that we create with you.

We've handled everything from putting in environmental systems, waste management systems and green building systems, and we make safety one of our top priorities. However, we do a lot more than just safety, as any of our clients can tell you.

At the end of the day, we're managers and problem solvers. The issue is that for many people, construction projects are an uncharted territory. They know what needs to get done, and they might even know most of the people that they need to call, but they are not sure how to handle things like city councils and safety inspections.

It may seem that a simple certification or the way that the site is set up should have nothing to do with how the project moves forward, but from long experience, we can tell you that something as "minor" as this can bring a project screeching to a halt. Once a construction project grinds to a halt, it takes a lot of work, a lot of time, a lot of effort and a lot of headache before it moves forward again!

A slowdown of this sort can lead to projects going way past their deadlines or, in a worst case, scenario, not getting completed at all. In all our years of construction management, we have never run into a client who was okay with this, and that is where we come in.

In the middle of a group of people who may not be communicating well and who may not know what it takes to make sure that things get done quickly, safely and under budget, we come in and we take responsibility. Even if you hire a group of talented contractors, you are looking at people from a wide variety of experiences and who all hold a very, very different skill set.

This skill set is what you need to get the project done, but it does not mean that they are going to coordinate well, and it doesn't mean that they have the skill that is necessary to help them get the proper certifications and to abide by the essential rules.

LETTING OUR TRACK RECORD SPEAK FOR ITSELF

Let's put it this way: what can you do in 10 weeks?

In ten weeks, we can build a Citroen dealership.

What can you do in three months?

In three months, we can come in to a situation with a troubled Peugeot dealership, fixing extensive issues with external cladding, and all while the full business was still in operation.

You can see that our top priority is customer satisfaction. Anyone can say that, but when we say it, we mean that we finish your project on time and on budget. We come in to assess the issue, we make sure that we have all the facts, and then we tell you what we can do and how long it takes.

It really is as simple as that. Your construction project takes up an enormous amount of energy, money and work, and if you are like our very satisfied clients, you cannot afford to waste a single bit of it. We help you make the most of your resources, and we do not permit any waste or any delay in getting your project out the door.

WE ARE CERTAINTY IN AN UNCERTAIN WORLD

Stop for a moment and think about your company's future. Whether you are thinking of a project that is meant to take place tomorrow or one that is going to be going up in a few years time, you are not going to progress without it. There reaches a point where you grow or you stagnate, and we're here to help you grow.

Life can be uncertain, but what we offer is certainty. We will tell you what can be done, what should be done, and what you can expect. When you enter a construction phase, your company is vulnerable in a way that it simply is not on a day to day basis. Suddenly, you have resources sunk into something that will not pay off until the project is done, and this is enough to make everyone nervous.

You've heard the horror stories, and coming up in the construction business, we've seen them as well. There has never been a time when construction isn't a risk, but what many people don't seem to understand is that it can be a managed risk.

At the end of the day, we're the people that you call when you want to make sure that your project goes well. There's a lot that can go wrong during a construction project, and not only do we prevent disaster, we also make sure that your project thrives.

Whether you've got construction on the mind and an empire to build, or you are contemplating a construction project that is designed to carry your company or property into the future, Smith and Madisha Construction will get you where you need to be.

Do yourself a favour and call us in when something needs to go up, go down or get improved, because we'll make sure that it happens and that it happens in the way that you want it to.

As a graduate of the University of Johannesburg, Alice Madisha holds a National Diploma in Building, and in addition that, she gained a B-tech degree in construction management from Tshwane University of Technology. When it comes to the construction industry, she can handle everything short of using a jack-hammer!

Jannie Smith has a National Higher Diploma in Building Science. He started his career with Basil Read and worked his way up through the various management levels of Basil the company, subsequently moving to Concor to be appointed a director of Concor Building in 2008. He has worked for a number of major clients including Rand Merchant Bank Properties, Investec, and the Mines Pension Fund.

At the helm of his own company, he successfully completed 3 major projects. His company merged with C-PRO CONSTRUCTION and he became a partner of the merged entity. Jannie has an enviable reputation for delivering prestigious projects for major clients on time, in budget and to the right quality, and far exceeding the expectations of his clients and his members of his professional team.

Find out more at: www.smithmadisha.co.za

Save My Relationship

The Master Plan for Creating an Amazing Relationship

CHRIS HART

Beata came to me with her relationship in tatters. Her boyfriend, Matt, had recently moved out of the flat they'd shared for five years, claiming that he no longer loved her. She thought they had been moving towards marriage and was utterly devastated, lost, and confused. She told me that I was her last option. I hear that a lot. Beata did not believe that she could rekindle the relationship with Matt. She thought it was a lost cause and that she was a lost cause, too. She was grasping at straws. I saw a woman whose self-esteem and confidence were at an all-time low. I saw a woman who was broken, emotionally. I saw a woman I could help.

I welcomed Beata with open arms. We sat down and, as I listened to her talk, I formulated an action plan for her to follow. She stuck with the plan, and with me, through many months of emotional healing and relationship work. I am thrilled to say that Beata and Matt are now happily married! Beata succeeded because she realized that she needed to work on healing herself as well as her relationship. Do not think this was an easy task for Beata. Some of the things I had to say were not easy for her to hear. My job is to be real. I will not tell you what you want to hear; I am not here to stroke your ego. Healing does not occur within denial. Beata had to do some difficult self-healing before we tackled her relational-healing with Matt. She is now extremely confident and aligned with her feelings. Furthermore, she is happily married and pursuing a life of "happily ever after."

If you are struggling with a failed, or near-failing, relationship, I can help you, too. My methods are not traditional self-help methodology, which focus on the mind. My methods focus on the heart; I concentrate on emotional guidance. You did not enter into your relationship using your mind. On the day you met your mate you did not think to yourself, "He seems like a good fit. I think I'll develop a loving relationship with this one." No, you did not use your mind; you used your heart. You met and fell in love. Therefore, you cannot solve relational problems with your head. This is an emotional problem that requires heart healing.

Maybe you wish to rekindle a romance that is dwindling, but you aren't quite ready for marriage. Such was the case with Talia, who came to me during a troubling time in her life. She was young and in love…or so she thought. Her boyfriend, Doug, had recently distanced himself from her. At first, he pulled away emotionally. He still hung out with her and took her out, but he seemed distracted and was not fully present with her. Eventually, he began making plans that did not include Talia. She was left feeling hurt and confused. Talia's thoughts began to take over her conscious moments with a constant barrage of questions: Was Doug the right choice for her? Should she wait for him to come around and decide what he wants and who he wants to be with? Should she move on and date someone else? Exactly what was he doing when he was not with her?

Talia's friends were divided. Some counseled her to not let Doug get away; they gave her ideas of how she could change herself to be more attractive to Doug. Others scoffed at that notion and told Talia she could do better than Doug, and counted off several other guys who'd already expressed interest in dating Talia. Talia's mother told her that "Things have a way of working themselves out" and to be patient. Talia's head was spinning from overthinking this situation.

Talia eventually got out of her own head and contacted me. After our first session, Talia was able to organize her thoughts and set them aside to focus on her heart. Soon she realized that she was not quite ready to give up on Doug. She was not sure if the relationship was one that would last forever, but she wanted to pursue it. So, we set to work.

I soon realized that Talia was harboring quite a bit of anger, not only towards Doug, but towards the friends who had been so quick to tell her what to do. Of course, this really means that Talia was angry with herself for allowing others to treat her this way. She denied this in the beginning; I had to be quite stern with her to enable her to see how she was allowing others to treat her. Talia was young, a college student, so her friends held a lot of influence over her. So often I find that people care more about what others think of them than what they think of themselves! Eventually, Talia came to see that she had to stop listening to others and only listen to me, and herself.

We put an action plan in place and Talia was able to examine her heart, rather than being lost in her thoughts all the time. After working with me, Talia was able to emotionally heal herself. She is now a much stronger young woman who has many close friends, yet thinks for herself. Thanks to my work, Doug has decided that he wants to continue his relationship with Talia. He is much more open with her about what he is wants. Talia and Doug are now happily dating and are excited to see where their relationship goes in the future.

When you utilize my methods you will find the last missing jigsaw piece that solves everything in your world of romance; that is, your relationship. I will enable you to regain your confidence and self-esteem by giving you the knowledge of what you can do to resolve your romantic problems. Many women come to me for help. My methods work because I am a man, therefore I think like a man. I can help women understand how their men think.

One of the first things a woman does when her relationship hits the rocks is to pick up the phone and call her closest friend or family member. After all, your friends will commiserate with you and offer you a shoulder to cry on. On the other hand, be cautious because your loved ones may soon begin to belittle your man or point out everything that was wrong with the relationship. This is no good! Whether they are correct or not, they are not in your shoes. They are not living your life, nor do they understand what you feel or what you want. You should stop listening to friends and family, especially if what they are saying does not align with your desires. They usually mean well, but cannot understand your relationship or your heart.

Once you stop listening to others, you must next stop overthinking. Putting an end to overthinking is the key! If you are hurting and mourning the loss of your love, you are thinking, thinking, thinking about what you can do to get him back, or what you wish you had done differently. You are spending too much time and energy thinking about your problems. All of this overthinking is surely affecting other areas of your life. Are you able to be productive at work? Or do make careless mistakes along the way because you are focused on your current loss. Are you fully present when someone else is talking to you? Or is your mind on your own problems that you are feverishly thinking about? Are you losing sleep due to overthinking? Overthinking about your current romantic problems leads to self-blame, loss of confidence, and a lack of awareness of the true nature of the problem. Two people usually share the blame when a relationship ends. When you overthink, you victimize yourself. Do not think like a victim. I will teach you how to become a victor. With my new way of thinking, you will be put back in control of your emotions.

Having control over your emotions is the key to victory. I will teach you how to have closure with the old self and to be the woman in control. Controlling your emotions can change you completely. You may not recognize this change in yourself, but others will see this metamorphosis and be inspired by you. People will be attracted to you because of your inner transformation. Learning to become the victor and think like a victor requires that you get real with yourself. You must look deeply into your own desires and motives to recognize things that need to be changed. Consider me your personal coach; I will "kick butt" if I sense that you are being too soft on yourself, just as any good coach does with his or her trainee. I want you to succeed, therefore I will not accept anything less than 100% from you. If you are just looking for someone who will stroke your ego and tell you that you are always right, you may wish to go back to your friends. I am not that person. I am the person who will affect real change in your life and in your relationships.

There is beautiful change to be had, if you are willing to make it. If my relationship were ending, I would be wondering what I could have done to change things or save the relationship. Regrets would always be there somewhere. Women with regrets cry. Do you have regrets? Successful women do not cry; they try. In fact, they make things happen. Women who take action have no regrets. You, too, can make things happen to solve your relationship problems.

When a woman comes to my practice, the first thing I ask her is this: Do you really want him back? This may sound like an empty question, but it is not. The answer to this question is incredibly important. Often, women do not know the true answer to this question when they first come to see me. If you only want him back in order to exact revenge on him for the way he treated you, my methods will not work. You must be sure that you want him back and that you want him back for the right reasons. The second question I ask is this: To what degree do you want this man back in your life?

Sometimes a woman comes to me and does not know the answer to those questions. I met with Carla and could tell right away that she was unsure about seeing me. She was unsure about many things. Once we cleared the air with incense and began to set aside her thoughts and focus on her heart, Carla realized that she held too much anger and resentment towards her boyfriend to continue a relationship with him. She had been blinding herself to this reality because she was afraid of what to do without him.

Carla was so afraid of being on her own that she was willing to chase after a failing relationship. She was so caught up in her thoughts that she did not even realize what this was doing to her heart. Carla was putting herself last and discounting her own feelings!

I quickly formulated an action plan for Carla. She chose not to pursue the failing relationship with her boyfriend; rather, she chose to pursue the failing relationship with herself. I got real with her and coached her on how to put herself first in her heart. This does not mean that she was to become a narcissist! No, this meant that she had to re-learn how to love and care for herself. She also had to learn to let go of her boyfriend. Using my methods, Carla was able to heal herself emotionally.

Carla recently contacted me to let me know that she is dating someone new. She is in love! She breathlessly told me how her new beau was the perfect match for her. I smiled to myself because I know he is the perfect match for her because she healed herself and was open to finding love.

Maybe you will decide that you do not want your man back in your life. Maybe you will decide that you want your man back for the right reasons and you realize to what degree you want him in your life. I can help you with both situations. When you work with me, I ask that you listen only to two people: yourself and me. Please do not think I am being conceited with this statement. If you are having a problem with a guy, listen to me. I do not say this to sound conceited, but I am a guy. Since I am a guy, I think like a guy. You need someone who thinks like a guy to help you with your guy. Furthermore, I have your best interest in mind. I have no preconceived notions about your relationship or whether the man is 'good enough' for you. I want what you want.

Listen to yourself. Have you been doing that? Or have you been overthinking the problem and assigning all kinds of blame to yourself? Listen to your authentic self. Do not allow others to influence your thoughts. It matters what you think and what you want, not what the others in your life think or want. Once you are ready to stop overthinking and blaming, you are ready for productive change.

I will share a bit of what I can do with you to save your relationship. First, I use incense to clear any negativity in the air. I know which incense to use that will combine the right energy with the right purpose of healing your relationship. Incense also prepares your mind for the process of healing your relationship. The incense I use will heighten your awareness, focus your thoughts, and bring about calm or healing energies during our work. When using incense to enhance energy, it provides assistance to direct your energy in a specific direction of self-healing. You will ultimately be able to alter your inner perceptions about yourself to create the life you want. Of course incense cannot do this alone, but it can help create or enhance the desired energies for our work together.

Along with incense, I use crystals in my practice. Crystals have the power to heal and attract if used wisely. Rose Quartz is a particularly good crystal for healing relationships, and is one that I use in my practice. Rose Quartz, also known as the Love Stone, is the stone of unconditional love; therefore, it is particularly powerful for healing broken relationships. Rose Quartz opens the heart chakra to encourage forgiveness and will, along with my counseling, help you let go of anger, resentment, jealousy, or any negative feelings you have towards your partner.

We begin with the first of two tests. These 'tests' will determine my unique action plan for your situation. The first test involves the use of imagery. Imagine your guy standing right in front of you. Take time to allow his image to materialize in your mind, noting details of his appearance. After you have the image of him in mind, ask yourself what colour you feel he has near his head area. Next, ask yourself what colour he has in his heart area. Finally, ask yourself what colour he has in his erogenous area. Take your time and allow the colours to materialize. Now take a look at yourself. What colours do you see in these areas for yourself? If you are struggling with this imagery while reading, do not lose heart. When you visit with me, I will guide you to accurately see the colours you have in mind for yourself and your partner.

Colour is, at its most essential, light and energy. People have been using colour, along with light and energy, to heal for thousands of years. Colour is also a form of nonverbal communication that influences emotion. There is a specific psychological response to each colour. Psychological effects have been observed relating to the following two main categories of colour: warm and cool. Warm colours, such as red, yellow, and orange, can spark a variety of emotions ranging from comfort and warmth to hostility and anger. Cool colours, such as green, blue and purple, often spark feelings of calmness and peace, as well as sadness or melancholy.

The colours you saw in the above exercise indicate your emotions regarding yourself and your mate. Your colour choices guide me in developing your personal action plan to harmonize the colours into the proper colour for a successful, loving relationship. If your colour choices indicate that your relationship is in real danger of ending, I can work with you to change the colours you see.

I will teach you to use your mind and emotions to align your proper colour with your guy. Along with incense and crystals, I utilize a picture of the person, since a photograph is an inner vibration of a person. Once you start working on your colours with me, relational changes occur quickly. A woman I counseled recently was able to complete an emotional bonding with her guy, even though he had moved out and ended the relationship. This couple is now married.

I hope that I have inspired you to take action to salvage a hurting relationship. If you are ready to take charge of your life and save your relationship, contact me through my website: www.loveguidance.co.uk. My hope is that reading this has been an awakening for you to see your own problems as they truly are, and to stop thinking like a victim. Through a session with me, you will be able to regain your strength and confidence to win him over. I will help you find closure with your old self and what has gone wrong in your past. Your new way of thinking will attract people to you and put you back in control of yourself and your emotions.

Do not be a woman with regret; be a woman in control.

Romancing Your Way Through Network Marketing

DORCAS TAY

"By three methods we may learn wisdom: first, by reflection, which is noblest; second, by imitation, which is easiest; and third by experience, which is the bitterest."
– Confucius

I started out in network marketing the way 99% of people do, with no clue what I was doing and no one to show me how. My results proved it. It was hard because I had this desire to make it big but lacked the knowledge and skills to make it work. I was determined to succeed but did not know how to get there.

I spent the next few years going from company to company hoping that each one would be THE ONE. If you have been in network marketing, you know exactly what I am talking about. You always think that the next company will be the magic one that takes you from zero to millions.

Throughout those years there was always one thing I did, and that was learning. I took advantage of every training session I could go to. I read books and watched videos. I devoured anything I could get my hands on.

As time went by something happened, I started to realize that the issue was not with the company, the products, the compensation plan, the team or the prospects. The problem was deep inside of me. I had spent years learning the skills I needed, but at the core of me, I did not honestly believe that I could be successful. I was blocking my goals and dreams from becoming a reality.

If you are reading this chapter, you are probably hoping for some magical revelation or formula that will guarantee instant success. But life does not work that way. There is no gidget, gadget or gizmo that is going to propel you to immediate results.

What I learned during that process changed me forever, and I am so thankful for it. I had self-limiting beliefs, and I was sabotaging myself at every step, subconsciously turning my beliefs into reality. This may sound strange to you, but it is true. No matter how big your desire is on the outside, if your subconscious has been conditioned to believe that you are not worth success, you will unconsciously do things to make what you believe reality and blame everything but yourself. You will block your own success.

Once I figured out what those beliefs were and changed my thinking, life started to become better. I immersed myself in changing those beliefs by attending numerous seminars, workshops, and personal development programmes. Indeed, investing in one's education and growth is wise and has a long-lasting impact on one's life.

From every failure, I learned precious lessons and so can you. If you feel like you are failing, do not nurse the guilt, embarrassment or blame. You can turn the failure into a learning experience.

Avoid blaming others or yourself. Doing so is like falling into quicksand. It will only entangle you deeper into emotional turmoil. The situation will become more complicated, and nothing good will be gained. Spend quiet time in retrospection, evaluate what happened, and embark on an action plan for how to perform better in the next opportunity.

Going through such a process is a necessary path of learning from failure and then trying again. Continually ask yourself, "What can be done differently in the next attempt?" and "Who can I learn from to do this better?" If you are not willing to evaluate and learn from past failures, then all those past experiences are a wasted journey.

WHAT I LEARNED IN NETWORK MARKETING

Over the years I have realized that being in network marketing is a lot like being in a relationship. When you understand all the stages, it will help you to get more results.

The first stage in network marketing is prospecting, which is akin to the dating stage. At this initial stage, you get to know the person who recruited you and the company they work for just like the first dates of a boy and a girl where they get to know each other. Both sides want to make the best impression on the other.

Prospecting is like the first attempt in dating. There is an air of curiosity and anticipation. The excitement is felt more in the first few dates. Thoughts of, "Oh, will Amy be the one for me? Will she be the girl of my dreams?" They flood the mind, and you get butterflies in your stomach.

This is very much the same when a new network marketer meets their first few prospects. Thoughts of, "Oh, will Amy be my downline? Will she be the ace in my team and bring in a lot of people?"

Everyone hopes to meet the ideal downline who will carry the baton, run the race and fight the good fight to the top. Ideally, when this happens, one can then relax and enjoy the sun and sea while passive income keeps flowing in. This is idealistic thinking.

Network marketing does not work this way, as many network marketers would like to have you believe. If you are hoping to meet your ace among your prospects, you are very likely chasing the Holy Grail. To be successful in network marketing, you had better first BE that ace and show the way through your actions and leadership. Just as a dating couple is wishing the other person is the ideal partner, one has to look inward and BE the ideal partner first.

Build genuine relationships with your prospects. Do not just recruit them and then leave the person to fend for him or herself.

As appalling as it is for a person to be used and then left to nurse their hurt and find their own recovery, so it is for someone to be brought into a network marketing company and then abandoned. In such a situation, people do feel betrayed, sore and regretful especially when personal savings were put into joining the network company. To truly build a team, one must diligently ensure the new downline completes the company's business training.

The important part at this stage is clear communication. You may want things from your leader and company that they cannot give, and they may want you to produce more results than you are capable of.

It is essential to let your leader know what you need and then listen and take what you can. Not all leaders are strong, and you may have to accept the fact that you will have to go other places for training. This is your business, and it is your responsibility - both for its growth and your personal success, not the success of others.

The next stage in network marketing is akin to a couple living together. Network marketers share the dream of financial and time freedom. They build the business together, spend time together at trainings, business presentations, and team bonding events. Leaders share a genuine interest in their downline's well-being and success. They work together as a team to achieve their objectives.

This is similar to couples living together, caring for each other, spending time together, and engaging and sharing common activities (meals, household chores, sports, charity work, etc.)

There are network marketers who neglect to build their new downline's knowledge about the products, the company, and the compensation plan. After signing up a new person, the network marketer simply leaves the new joiners to themselves or refers them to call the company's customer care hotline should they have any questions or difficulties.

The network marketer goes on to his next prospect, too busy to spend time with his team's downlines. The new joiner, meanwhile, feels frustrated, abandoned, taken advantage of by the upline. This can be paralleled to an absent father or mother in a family where the kids and household matters are left to one partner. The other partner is too busy at work, or with other activities, to spend time with the family. As we know, such behavior can adversely affect the spouse and children in the long term.

If you want to build strong customers, team members, and businesses, then you must put time into the relationships; you must nurture them. For customers this means providing good customer service, taking care of their needs, providing product information and caring about them.

For your team members, you must spend time with them and train them. You may not know all the answers yet but be there for them. When you do not know the answer, find out for them. Encourage them to come to company events and training. Give them recognition, whether verbally, socially or in the form of prizes. Let them know that they are valued, and they will want to stay with you and build their business.

It is easy at this stage to think that you do not need to give them any attention since they are already 'living with you.' This is the most important stage because the initial excitement has worn off and this is when the true commitment begins.

You are married. Now what?

This is the stage where things start to grow because the level of commitment is there and established. You have developed a good, strong customer base of people who order regularly, and you have built a stable team who want to work. Life gets easy or so you think. While things are easier when you reach this stage, it is tempting to start neglecting everything because you have already made it. Why bother when everything is running smoothly? Like a marriage, if you neglect your marriage, it will decay over time, and eventually, you will not have a marriage anymore.

If you want to stay successful, you must continue to do the things that you did when growing your business. You must be involved and help others to grow too. Continuously give encouragement, rewards and recognition. If you continue to do these things, your business will flourish.

A marriage also produces children, so make babies and more babies! Isn't it exciting how overjoyed a couple feels when they have a baby (particularly the first child)? The happiness even outflows to relatives and friends.

It is the same in network marketing when you have your first sign-up. You are elated as are your uplines and those supportive of your business. However, just as a baby needs to be nourished and nurtured, so does each and every one of your downlines. Just as responsible parenting is crucial for every child's development so is the training and development of your team members in network marketing.

Divorce

Sometimes, you join a company and it is just not the right fit. Maybe you have no support whatsoever from your leader, or even worse, they are making things difficult for you.

Maybe you realize that you cannot support the products with your full heart and they do not give the promised results. Or perhaps you poured out all your effort, passion and belief in the company and products but the company becomes tardy in payment or even stops paying as they should. No matter what the reason, there are times when you need to leave a company.

My suggestion is, if this is your situation, then you need to leave peaceably. Let people know why you are leaving, however, do it in such a way that you keep the relationship in good standing. You never know when that relationship will help you in the future.

What is next? Some people may choose not to stay in network marketing. Maybe they are too hurt or found it too hard.

But...

If your desire is to truly build an amazing business, then you need to find a new company. Take your time and do your research. You have experience now and can make a better decision.

One thing that can never be in network marketing is fear. In the same way that fear will kill a relationship, it will also bring death to your business. Yes it can be hard, especially if you have been burnt before, but each company and leader are different. You have to give them the benefit of the doubt when joining.

Talk to people in the company. Find out who you want to be your leader. Find out about their events and go to them. See what the company is like before you join.

Is network marketing worth it? Of course it is. Perhaps, like me, you may have tried network marketing with little or no success and instead ended up spending money on the products. However, I did enjoy the events and getting to know more people.

Like any other business, you have to invest time and energy for a period of time to bring it to where you want it to be. It is a journey that will not only grow you as a person but will also enrich your life. In some unseen way, all these experiences have helped you become a wiser and more fulfilled you.

The following are tips to help you with your network marketing business. I call them the 12 C's of Network Marketing.

Compatibility. Get to know the person who is recruiting you and find out whether both of you can work well together (know who you are going to bed with). Do not simply join anyone who buys you a coffee (you are not so cheap).

Commitment. Look for people with whom you want to build a long-lasting relationship (enter into a marriage) and who will not just recruit and disappear (have a fling).

Camaraderie. Work together with a passionate force to achieve common goals, no matter what (stick through thick and thin in a relationship).

Communication, Compliments, and Complaints. Take time to know your prospect (know your life partner). Serve each other (a loving husband and wife relationship).

Consideration and Compassion. Do not look at every person you see on the street or anywhere as a prospect (not every person you meet will be desirous to go to bed with you).

Confidence and Ceaseless Passion. Commit your time, energy and effort to grow the size of your team (every new addition of a baby into the family brings great joy and fulfilment).

Celebrations. Create memories of happy times by celebrating achievements, special occasions and holidays (a couple's relationship is strengthened as they spend special happy moments and occasions together).

Charity. Do deeds of charity and incorporate social responsibility as a team to create more bonding, fulfilment, fun, and meaning while earning money (a couple is more fulfilled while looking beyond themselves to serve others in the community).

You can succeed in network marketing if you are willing to put in the time and effort and become the LEADER you want others to be to you.

If you have enjoyed reading this Chapter, do pass it on to someone you know who will also benefit from it.

I encourage you to continually seek learning and improving yourself in whatever you are focusing on. You can only become better.

In my book "LEARN AND BE ENRICHED. CREATE YOUR LIFE THROUGH LIFELONG LEARNING", I share personal life stories with powerful messages that will move you to be more, experience more and contribute more.

My book is available on www.amazon.com and www.dorcastay.com.

Are you curious to know what business I am up to now? Simply drop an email to dorcas.tay@gmail.com or go to www.dorcastay.com and grab your bonus gift today!

Enter Into a Passionate Relationship with Your Own Life

SILVANA AVRAM

Have you ever wondered whether there is more to life than meets the eye? Do you feel that despite all your achievements true fulfilment still eludes you?

Join me on this transformational journey where you will learn to see yourself and your life in a different light.

- You will find out how to ask the right questions.
- You will learn to identify the main reason why you find yourself trapped in the same vicious circle.
- You will redefine the true meaning of being and uncover the source of deep fulfilment.
- You will be able to decide whether you are ready to embark on the journey to personal fulfilment.

My passionate plea to you is to allow this introduction to the secret of lasting fulfilment to work as a powerful catalyst for you. Should you want to explore the topics addressed here in more depth I invite you to read my book "Being You And Loving You – The Ultimate Guide To Fulfilment" – where I guide you through twelve life changing steps to true fulfilment. Together with the book you will also find plenty of free materials, insights and support at www.BeingYouAndLovingYou.com

It is the aim of this chapter to empower you to start your journey to true fulfilment. Are you ready? Let's dive in!

YOUR JOURNEY TO FULFILMENT STARTS WITH ASKING THE RIGHT QUESTIONS

"The Universe contains three things that cannot be destroyed; Being, Awareness and LOVE"

— Deepak Chopra

"What is the meaning of life?" Human beings have searched for an answer to this question for millennia. Sages, philosophers, religious figures and scientists have all put forward their hypotheses, and each interpretation added yet another nuance to a mystery that remains as fascinating and as alluring as it has always been.

So: "Why are we here?" And why is it that this most important question of all is also one of the most avoided? Perhaps we have long accepted that there is no answer to it. Perhaps facing this question feels so…unsettling that we prefer to bury it under more…urgent matters. Like finding a job and paying the next bill.

I put to you another possibility. I believe that "Why are we here?" is indeed an unanswerable question. At least for the time being. And so is *"What is the meaning of life?"*

Why? Because they are too vast...and too vague!

Does that mean I am advising you to drop the questioning altogether and simply get on with your life? No, not at all! Not if you want to live a joyous, meaningful life. Not if you are looking for true fulfilment. In fact, if this is what you are after, it is vitally important to keep questioning.

But you must learn to ask the right questions.

I believe that each one of us must start with the more manageable "Why *am I* here?" or "What is the meaning of *my* life?"

I believe that each one of us must take responsibility for our own answers.

You see, when you allow someone else to answer these questions for you, you give away your power (and with that your responsibility). You may like a particular answer/ philosophy for a while and you may find it resonates with you – you may even dedicate your life to promoting it – but it will still not be yours – and as such it will not fully transform your life, it will not bring you the fulfilment you crave. You may read as many books as you want and you may attend endless wonderful seminars...They will all help you feel good for a while and you are sure to get some valuable insight. But no person and no book can truly change your life for you. Only when you find the strength and the courage to stay with the question of meaning long enough to allow for your own answer to be born in you, will you find the infinite joy and freedom that come from knowing. It is only *your own* answer that will truly transform *your life*. It is owning that answer that brings true fulfilment.

If your life is a riddle, the only way to fully - fill it… is to find your own answer to it.

Now that you know where to start…how do you actually do it?

You can find your own answer by asking the right questions, either on your own or by engaging in a philosophical dialogue with friends and other people interested in the same quest for meaning. You must be patient and tenacious, and not give up at the first signs of exhaustion or disappointment. After all, the question of meaning is the most challenging question of all, and many choose to avoid it altogether. But if you stay with it, if you make it an intrinsic part of your journey, sooner or later you will be rewarded.

You will not be alone in your endeavour. One of the most famous of the Delphic maxims inscribed in the pronaos (forecourt) of the Temple of Apollo at Delphi, Ancient Greece, and quoted by many, most famously by Socrates as the main character in Plato's dialogues, was *"Know Thyself"*. Through the ages there have been many who have embarked on this arduous journey.

Today, there is a modern variant of the life-transforming dialogues left to posterity by Plato: the coaching dialogue. The Philosopher is replaced by the more modest Coach. They are similar, however, in that the Coach, like the Greek philosopher but unlike a religious figure or a mentor, is not providing the answers. Instead, she or he is merely providing you with the right questions, gently challenging you when you go off track and often holding a symbolic mirror in which you start to see your true reflection and find your own answers.

It is a true measure of our 21st Century's *Age of Knowledge* that Coaching has become such an accessible experience. Perhaps this is a sign that more and more amongst us are ready and willing to stay with the question of meaning and find the true purpose of our lives. Perhaps more and more people are ready to embark on the journey to true fulfilment. Are you?

BEING SUCCESSFUL IS NOT THE SAME AS SUCCEEDING AT BEING

"What makes you think human beings are sentient and aware? There's no evidence for it. Human beings never think for themselves, they find it too uncomfortable. For the most part, members of our species simply repeat what they are told – and become upset if they are exposed to any different view. The characteristic human trait is not awareness but conformity.."

— Michael Crichton

"I am a human being, not a human doing. Don't equate your self-worth with how well you do things in life. You aren't what you do. If you are what you do, then when you don't...you aren't."

— Dr. Wayne Dyer

Before we proceed to consider what your journey to true fulfilment might look like when you embark on a path of enquiry and examination, I would like you to briefly stop and take a look at your life right now.

Do you love your life? Do you love yourself? Do you feel deep gratitude and awe about who you are? Do you feel blissful, fulfilled and radiant, sharing your wisdom and your light with everyone else, in compassion?

Chances are that you don't.

Chances are that you don't even believe this is possible!!

But if it were possible, would you like to feel like this? Would you like to live your life with absolute joy, and share your happiness with others?

I hope your answer to that last question is yes.

If it is, you have already taken the first step to fulfilment.

You see, most people have already given up on personal fulfilment. Most people have somehow fallen into the trap of believing that there is nothing more to life than work, duty, supporting family and friends, and the occasional recreation. It may sound incredible, but most people have convinced themselves that life is more about sacrifice and suffering than about being happy. If asked, of course everyone would say they want to be happy. Yet most people spend their lives doing things that take them farther and farther away from being joyful and fulfilled.

Most people spend most of their lives *doing* things. In fact doing so many things that they don't have the time to stop and ask *why* they are doing them.

Most people spend their lives doing so many things that they forget to Be.

But how can I forget to be? I hear you ask.

What else is there to 'being' that I haven't got already? Is it not enough that I am…alive? How can I be …being? How can I Be more?

You see…rocks and trees and animals are too. They exist. Life flows through them and expresses through them without encountering much opposition. They are pure expressions of life.

And so are we. Except for the fact that we also have the wonderful gifts of thought, of mind…of consciousness.

I want you to consider that maybe, just maybe, for us humans it is not enough to be alive, to truly Be. If it were, we would all be happy – or at least at ease. We would not ask questions. We would not search for more.

What makes us different is that we have the gift of being able to be aware of being. It is this gift, and whether or not we choose to use it, that makes all the difference.

In order to truly Be as a human being you must be aware of who you are – of your potential. You must get involved in "being", become responsible for your "being", become the co-creator of your life.

When, on the other hand, we choose not to use the gift of awareness, we spend most of our lives doing things, being alive without truly being aware of the mystery, the complexity and the beauty of our being. We allow doing to take over, we throw ourselves into doing with a vengeance, seeking solace in temporary achievements that often leave us emptier than before.

Why and how does this happen? When we live without fully being present to our own lives, to our own being, we function on automatic pilot much of the time. Most of the functions we perform require so little of our conscious input that we get used to being disengaged. It's easier. We do the minimum and we get by. If we are "lucky" we can spend our whole life without having to account for the huge lack of …presence in it. For the most part, everyone is doing the same, and we are covered. No one will know. No one will dare ask.

But is that truly "lucky"? Is our life really about "getting by"?

If it were, mere survival would qualify as fulfilment. You would already and at all times feel fulfilled. Yet most of us know deep down inside our hearts that our lives must be more than just survival.

Perhaps our life is about success?

The difference between success and fulfilment is that success, as it tends to be defined, is still at the level of doing. You can become successful by following instructions and still staying on autopilot. In fact, the more autopilot-friendly the system you follow, the more successful you probably are in that particular area.

It is a common mistake to equate success with fulfilment. Many people who do, realize that success has not brought them the fulfilment they wished for. Many of these people spend years wondering where they went wrong and what's missing.

Our society seems to conspire to push us towards a narrowly defined form of success that rarely allows any space for true fulfilment. In other words, our misinterpretations are not entirely our fault. We are taught from early on to play by the (widely accepted) rules. We trust our parents and our teachers, and we unwittingly follow in their footsteps. We keep ourselves busy doing so many things that we have little time for self-exploration or personal inquiry, for Being. It is this restless drive for doing more and more that slowly but surely derails us from the only achievement that matters: understanding, accepting and expressing – in fact Being - our true self. Unless we stop to ask the right questions we don't even realise what we are missing.

To sum it up, success in doing cannot lead to fulfilment, for the simple reason that it involves operating at a different level.

To achieve true fulfilment you must operate at the level of Being.

It is not being successful at doing that will make you feel fulfilled.

To be fulfilled you must succeed at Being.

* * * *

So far we have learnt that in order to be fulfilled you must start by asking the right questions: "What is the meaning of my life?" "Why am I here?"

Tackling these and similar questions of meaning helps you become aware: aware that there is more to life than meets the eye; aware that as a human being it is not enough to be alive...Nor is it enough to be doing many things.

We then looked at what happens when you don't ask these questions. When you avoid questioning the true meaning of your life you get sucked into a life of endless doing with very little time for Being – and hence, with very little or no chance of feeling fulfilled.

For most people the question of meaning is an intimidating one, and one they'd rather put aside. After all, why take responsibility for one's life when it seems easier to just get by? Many people "succeed" in avoiding this question altogether. They also miss the opportunity of living deeply fulfilling, joyful lives. For others, something happens that forces them to wake up to it. It could be an unexpected turn of fate, a tragic event, even a major bonus, like winning the lottery, that pushes them to take a deeper look in the mirror. At those times they discover that there is a whole new dimension to 'being' that they were completely ignoring before. It is then up to them to embark on a journey of discovery that should ultimately lead them to true fulfilment.

There is, of course, a more natural, organic way that comes when you simply decide to take responsibility for your life and actively explore the gifts it promises to offer. You do it because you realize this is the only way you are going to feel truly happy and fulfilled. You do it because you want to be a co-creator in your life and express your full potential.

Along the way you may need the help of a friend, a sage or a coach – and you may be able to help others – but ultimately each one of us must find our own answers in order to express the true richness of our lives.

Once you are on the path to fulfilment there is no going back. You taste the ecstasy of being alive. Everything thereafter is a miraculous discovery, a wonderful adventure, a self-affirming deed and a deeply fulfilling expression of who you are. You have been kissed by life.

TRUE FULFILMENT COMES FROM AN AUTHENTIC AND LOVING RELATIONSHIP WITH YOUR LIFE

"The first step toward change is awareness. The second step is acceptance."

— Nathaniel Branden

We have established that in order to find true fulfilment you must be able to start with the right question and you must be able and willing to stay with it until you find your own answer. This is no easy journey. But it is the only one that will get you to true fulfilment. And as such, it is the most exciting journey of all.

If you are looking for deeper fulfilment, if you have started to realise that fulfilment will not come from doing more "stuff", chances are that you are already awakening to the possibility of an infinitely richer you. It does not matter how long it took you to get to this point. What matters is that you are ready: ready to embark on the beautiful, empowering, liberating and ultimately fulfilling journey of Being; ready to Be. Now.

Congratulations! Let the journey begin!

* * * *

As a coach, I can never get tired of seeing my clients find true joy and meaning in their lives. It often feels as if I watch them learn how to fly. And when they take off on their own…The sense of unlimited potential, freedom and happiness that comes with finding your own answer to the mystery of life is truly indescribable. One must experience it to be able to understand it.

But, if you will allow me, I would like to share with you what you might expect along the way.

There are two essential ingredients that will ensure a successful journey.

1. In order to be fulfilled you must first learn to Be.
2. Then you must learn how to Love Being.

As we touched upon earlier, truly Being requires presence and awareness.

True fulfilment comes when you and your life become one. When you live passionately…fully. To be one with life you must first wake up to Being; you must be aware of who you really are.

To start with, this will involve exploring your strengths, your talents, your gifts. It will mean looking at what makes you *you*, what makes you unique. In case you are already backing off in fear, rest assured. Every one of us is unique. Your special features, your memories and stories, your thoughts and feelings, your desires and dreams…all these make you a world unto itself, a uniquely beautiful expression of life, an exquisite original work of art in constant motion. There is no one else in the entire universe like you. There has never been and there will never be! You just have to muster the courage to embrace this truth! And allow it to transform you! It will help to have someone else hold the mirror, but once you learn to look at yourself in this way you will be able to see your life in a different light.

(To learn more about how you can embrace and celebrate your uniqueness visit www.SilvanaAvram.com)

It will then be important to find ways to truly express who you are; to listen to your heart and let it teach you everything you had tried to forget. Becoming aware of your thought patterns and connecting with your deepest emotions will enable you to re-define yourself. Then you can move one step further and try your hand at re-creating who you are. Being you is the gift you were given. Accepting this gift and then bettering it will be the gift you give back to life. How wonderful. This is pure creation. It's a miraculous process. Let it be fun!

At this point you should be ready to start thinking of how you could share your gift with others. This will become your purpose. That's when the real magic begins. And with it, true joy.

This is the point on your journey when your love relationship with life truly begins. The intimate loving relationship that you have managed to build with yourself expands into a passionate love affair with your life.

Now that you have become the co-creator of your life you must allow yourself to fall in love with your creation. You and your life must become one. This means moving from living your life into allowing your life to live, to express through you. You must be in awe of your life, you must respect it and cherish it and place it above anything else. Because your life is your gift to yourself and to the world. Because your life is the most intimate expression of who you are.

Loving your life is acknowledging and loving the infinite potential that you are. Loving your life with passion will teach you how to love every life with passion – will help you connect with every other life in compassion and joy. Knowing that you have expressed the best of you gives you the licence to feel free, to feel happy, to feel fulfilled.

When you live your life with this intensity there is a point where you will have to lose yourself to find yourself. That is when you must confront your deepest fear. Just as you have learnt to love yourself you must prepare to lose yourself. This is your ultimate act of sacrifice. You understand that your life does not belong to you. And this makes you love it even more. Now living your best possible life truly becomes your mission – and the only measurement of feeling true fulfilment.

You are now close, very close in fact, to fulfilment. You have already had glimpses of it – and you have started to feel its presence more and more poignantly. It is a mysterious, evasive feeling but one that is constant, and constantly making you blush. It permeates your life like a subtle perfume, like the light filling a room – like the presence of joy.

Your wonderful ability to be has now become a living example for others to see. By being you and fulfilling your mission you gift the world with your presence, and your life is the very proof of your fulfilment.

You inspire, you touch other lives and you share your wisdom and your joyful awareness with ease.

You live your life with the profound and blissful awareness of having achieved true fulfilment and the immense gratitude of having been able to do so.

* * * *

How does that feel? I hope you were able to get a glimpse of what it might mean to walk the journey to fulfilment. Often the transformation that takes place is difficult to put into words.

Suffice it to say that in this magical process you and your life will be completely transformed.

You enter a true partnership with life. You fall in love with your life and you become a co-creator of your life. That is the true meaning of being one with life. You live passionately – vibrantly. You express through your life and your life expresses through you.

To love being, to be in love with your life, is to step beyond being you into the miraculous field of living your life in service to Life – of giving your life as a gift back to Life. Everything you do at this level enriches you and enhances your life while affirming Life itself.

True fulfilment comes from being authentic and accomplishing your potential – thus fulfilling and honouring the unique opportunity that your life is.

(Explore more and get inspired with the wealth of insights and materials on the topic of being you, loving you and transcending you…that you will find at: www.BeingYouAndLovingYou.com)

LIVING A FULFILLING LIFE: IF NOT NOW, WHEN?

"Waking up is not a selfish pursuit of happiness, it is a revolutionary stance, from the inside out, for the benefit of all beings in existence."

– Noah Levine

We have explored together what it takes to embark on the journey to personal fulfilment.

We saw that it all starts with asking the right questions. We looked at what might happen when we fail to ask these questions. Then we had a glimpse at what to expect once we embark on this journey. I suppose the only question left is…Are you in?

You see… You either are or you aren't feeling fulfilled right now. And if you aren't, you are faced with a serious choice. True personal fulfilment involves presence and passion. You can't tell your life "I will live you tomorrow" or "I will love you tomorrow." You can't tell your mission, your purpose "I will be with you later." You have to be ready, open to it now. You have to commit to living your best possible life now.

The journey to fulfilment is not the easiest. It does require courage, honesty, a deep sense of wonder, the desire to overcome fears and the capacity to accept life's ephemeral and mysterious nature – and love it all the more for it.

To truly know fulfilment you must make the transition from living at the doing level to living at the Being level. Being successful has nothing to do with being fulfilled. Succeeding at Being has everything to do with it.

To truly succeed at Being you must go on a journey of self-discovery, and learn to celebrate your uniqueness, your richness, your unique expression, your feelings. You must learn to become a conscious co-creator of your life and then find the best ways to share your creation.

With this you move towards learning to love yourself and falling in love with your life. Once you learn to love yourself you must overcome your fear of losing yourself. This gives you the freedom to share yourself with the world.

By doing this you become an inspiration to others. You share the light of awareness with others. Finally you give back your life to Life with and for others – and in this you find ultimate fulfilment.

I don't know of a more wondrous journey – or one that is more worth it. You have been invited. The door has been opened for you. But only you can walk this journey and make your life the most extraordinary adventure of all. It is your life. Will you make it your fulfilment?

FINAL THOUGHT

If these pages have inspired you, you are probably ready to embark on the journey to fulfilment. Sometimes all we need is for someone to point the way. At other times we need someone to hold our hand as we learn how to fly on our own. I believe that Coaching can do that.

I believe that we live in a world where holding hands and learning from each other is soon becoming the norm. It is the only way in which we will be able to move forward. It is the only way in which we will learn, together, to truly Be. To be in love with our lives and to honour our potential. To find deep and lasting fulfilment. To share our richness and our beauty with everyone else, in joy. You can do it! See you there!

* * * *

Silvana is a successful Inspirational Coach, philosopher, writer and teacher.

More than anything else Silvana is a passionate human being driven by a deep commitment to create a better, happier world for everyone. She founded Life Coaching with Silvana to reach out and make her own contribution through empowering individuals to embrace and fulfil their potential, follow their dreams and live life with joy and gratitude. Silvana currently lives in the UK and divides her time between writing, coaching, group coaching, teaching, travelling, supporting humanitarian projects and conducting workshops and seminars.

To get in touch with Silvana, to know more about her Coaching practice, her projects and the events she organizes visit www.LifeCoachingWithSilvana.com

To get her book "Being You and Loving You – The Ultimate Guide To Fulfilment" together with free materials and more insights into the topic of fulfilment visit: www.LifeCoachingWithSilvana.com

The Love Drug

Your Lifetime Supply of Metaphysical Pharmaceuticals

WILMA DAVID AGUILA

First of all, let me begin by saying I am an advocate of mental wellness and healthy living. In my sixteen years in Canada, I have been privileged to have worked in the pharmaceutical industry, innovating and developing drugs, and in pharmacies where I've had direct interaction with patients. I've learned through these interactions how wide a knowledge gap exists in regard to the awareness of the medicines we take. There's a gap with respect to what a medicine's focus and intention is relative to what the patient may want it to be. Interesting assumptions are made about what the medication may offer, sometimes beyond what the manufacturer intended, all in the search for normalcy and wellbeing.

I'm sure you know of someone who at some time or another resorted to the use of synthetic drugs to self-medicate. For example, some may use pain medications to deal with feelings of heartache or pain associated with failure, fear, anxiety or let-down. Sleeping pills may be used beyond treatment for insomnia, to deal with anxiety or stress. I've encountered people who believe an elevated heart rate that recurs has to be a symptom of a disease, when a little prodding reveals stress as the main culprit. Let's not forget the power of the internet, and how many of us use it to self-diagnose: perhaps the most detrimental factor that drives self-medicating.

The truth is that most people fail to listen to and put faith into the power of their inner voice and its influence on wellness and self-care. In this context, self-care refers to any necessary human regulatory function under an individual's control. There is no intention here to contradict the use of pharmaceutical drugs to treat a true condition or ailment as diagnosed by a medical practitioner, rather it's my intent to emphasise an awareness of metaphysics, and adopting it as a way of life. This chapter will explore a system that utilizes a series of phases to incorporate into your lifestyle and mindset that may be used to improve wellness.

We all have an opportunity to utilize self-care and awakening to help deal with things like depression and other mental illness. I have, many times, referred to an acronym I read once: C.R.E.A.M—Consciousness Rules Everything Around Me. It's part of the idea that we draw conclusions, right or wrong, from what we observe or are influenced by in our lives. If it's common sense to train our mind to focus on the positives and make it habit, then why are we not all doing it? It's also part of the idea that cognitive tools are often enough to remedy depression and other mental illnesses. Drugs should be a last resort.

Before we continue, I should tell you that my specialty is guiding people to experience the root meaning and cause of the problem(s) they are facing and to bring inner healing to the root emotions involved. My passions are focused listening, helping people with anxiety, and offering support and guidance in a loving and nurturing way. I also support women's health and act as a mental health coach to help those who are suffering with low energy, tiredness, etc.

Think about the metaphor of "moon phases." The idea is that we go through phases just as the moon does. Thinking of life in phases can help us to stay on track without feeling overwhelmed. For example:

- New Moon: this is a time to set intentions, choose new beginnings, embark upon new adventures and make positive changes

- Waxing Moon: now focus on growth, learning, creativity, healing and transformation

- Full Moon: complete the achievement of your goals, harvest what you have sown and protect what you have; it's also a time to focus on cleansing

- Waning Moon: open up, release and let go

Refer to and use the moon phases in your life to consistently reflect on the following ten steps to self-care: After all, the moon is a steady reminder that is always present and looking down on you from the heavens every night. Associating the moon phases to these ten steps is a roadmap to wellness and healthy living.

DRUGS

If you are someone who is troubled by drug use, the moon phase analogy can definitely help you. Before getting into the moon phase analogy here's a little background.

Misuse of prescription drugs is defined as the taking of a medication in a manner or dose other than prescribed; taking someone else's prescription, even if for a legitimate medical complaint such as pain; or taking a medication to feel euphoria (i.e., to get high). The term nonmedical use of prescription drugs also refers to these categories of misuse.

The three classes of medication most commonly misused are:

- opioids—usually prescribed to treat pain
- central nervous system [CNS] depressants—used to treat anxiety and sleep disorders
- stimulants—most often prescribed to treat attention-deficit hyperactivity disorder (ADHD)

Prescription drug misuse can have serious medical consequences. Increases in prescription drug misuse over the last two decades are reflected in increased emergency room visits, overdose deaths associated with prescription drugs, and treatment admissions for prescription drug use disorders, the most severe form of which is addiction. The percentages of prescription abusers seeking medical help is estimated to be in the double digits. Unintentional overdose deaths involving opioid pain relievers have more than quadrupled since 1999 and have long outnumbered those involving heroin and cocaine.

Now if you incorporate the moon phase analogy:

New Moon: make positive changes. First step is a desire to change. You need to believe you are at risk of jeopardizing your own wellbeing if you continue on this path. You need to believe there is a solution and a way out. If you could have done it on your own, chances are you would have done it already. Seek professional counseling. Find a branch of Narcotics Anonymous (designed with the same model as Alcoholics Anonymous), do whatever you can to reduce and eventually end your drug use. Change your focus. Look to substitutes for non-medicinal healthy substitutes to get you that high. Get high on life: it's the quintessential end, isn't it? What we're all searching for? If you aren't happy, look for the reasons why, jot them down, write what needs to change, set a plan to achieve it and, most importantly, work at it tirelessly. Make work and effort the substitute for the high. Bottom line... only YOU can do something about it.

Focus on growth, which is the Waxing Moon. There are many ways to overcome the negatives in life. A psychologist or psychiatrist can offer up cognitive tools or you can try some of the following:

a) Turn your back on darkness or negativity and look to the light. This can mean different things for different people, but the idea is to drive the darkness away, as dark cannot exist where there is light. Personally, I am always looking for the beauty in life. It gives me great joy. I find this beauty in nature, in art, and in the people I meet. I also have the good fortune of having the light of the Lord with me each day. The trick is to look wherever you can find something to lighten your mind and push away dark thoughts that can drag you down into self-abuse.

b) Consciously choose your thoughts and emotions. Life has no meaning unless we put it there. You have the free will to choose to think and feel what you want, no matter what is happening in your life. It's a simple choice that gives you great power. Choose yes or no, forward or backward, up or down, left or right, this thought versus that thought. Whatever the situation is, you can always boil it down to a single choice like good versus bad or light versus dark.

c) Emotion is a wild horse you must learn to tame and ride. Whenever any overwhelming emotion visits you, ring it in and ride it out. Sooner or later it will run out of steam and you will regain control. This kind of focus will take your mind off whatever actions you may have been contemplating when fueled by emotion. This approach will put you in idle mode while you take the wild ride on the stallion of your emotion. It's a safe way to deal with emotions that have the potential to harm. Emotions drive our actions, giving us the impetus to turn our thoughts into behaviours. Better to calm the wild horse and act calmly yourself than let it loose to wreak havoc in your life.

Harvest your efforts (Full Moon). Make sure you take the time to reflect over the past weeks and months to assess and identify where and how you've grown or changed. Celebrate these victories and record what has worked and what hasn't worked. Leap forward and complete some of the goals you have set. Now you'll have even more to celebrate. Reward yourself. Each of us has their own personal idea of what constitutes a reward. You may go out for a nice dinner, take a mini-vacation, or buy that book or movie you've wanted. It could be something as simple as stop for an ice cream cone. You are limited only by your imagination.

Waning Moon: open up, release, let go. Remember that even though you determine the right choice once, you may have to recommit to that same choice numerous times. It takes time to overcome habits and beliefs. The key to developing the long-term behaviours that are necessary for your success is to open up and let go of the old behaviours. You don't need them anymore, so dig them up and show them the light of day. Begin to understand that you are the source of all your thoughts, emotions and actions, and that this gives you complete control—if you are willing to take it. Remember that the drug behaviours are just that: they are behaviours you are choosing, not things that are happening to you. You can just as easily choose a better behaviour in this moment, in the next moment and so on. Eventually you will break the addiction—I guarantee it.

For personal assistance through mental health coaching, please contact **me@wilmadavidaguila.com**.

THE STRUGGLE IS REAL

Don't get me wrong. The struggle people with mental or physical issues have is very real and often requires the help of prescription drugs. The purpose of this chapter is not to deal with the current level of non-medical use of prescription drugs. Instead, I'm directing my words to those who are misusing legitimate prescriptions. These could be people who believe they are sick when what they really need is to learn some tough life skills, or those who began using for legitimate reasons but are now using for the sake of using. None of you deserve to have the small deviations from the set course translate into the huge monkey on your back. What is required is the offer of nonjudgmental help to learn how to deal with the underlying issues that have gotten you to the point where you are now. Psychiatrists, psychologists and some social workers can offer cognitive tools and other life skills to deal with what has, up until now, been dealt with by the misuse of prescription drugs.

The New Moon is a wonderful time to set new goals and make positive changes. To be a useful tool, goal setting must follow a set pattern:

1. The goal must be specific. Not "I am going to stop using drugs," but "I am going to stop using morphine within 30 days, beginning tomorrow morning and with the help of my doctor."

2. The goal must be timely. There's no point in setting a goal for three months from now. It needs to be something you can accomplish today. That's why you always hear about people breaking goals down into "baby steps" or "little bites." A goal is attainable by taking a certain pathway and then making constant course corrections to make sure you stay on that pathway. If a plane or a boat didn't use this same method, they would never reach their desired destination—because small deviations can take them many hundreds of miles off course. So ... take on your goal by making many small decisions and actions designed to get you where you ultimately wish to be, today.

3. You must take massive action. Reverse engineer your goals into their smallest achievable tasks, then act upon them with great vigour. Take the shotgun approach: one shot covers a larger area so as to improve the odds of hitting your target. You can do the same thing. Take as many different actions as you can think of to achieve the goal at hand. Then do the same for the next and the next, until you get to where you want to be.

4. A goal should be something you're passionate about achieving. You can't get anywhere on an empty gas tank. Neither can you achieve a goal if you are emotionally bereft. Emotions tend to move us to action, especially if they are supportive or positive in nature.

The Waxing Moon is a time for focusing on healing, growth and transformation. The very act of setting and achieving goals will teach you and bring you growth. But it is up to you to use the things you learn so as to promote healing and, ultimately, transformation. You must actively focus on change. Why? People just naturally harbour change. It's in our DNA, going back to times when change meant injury or death. The problem is that, today, most change is not injurious. Change is actually beneficial in many ways, and embracing it often uncovers opportunities you might never have otherwise imagined. Focus on transformation. It's a good thing.

The Full Moon is marked by the harvesting of your efforts, the achievement of your big goals. Now is a good time to look at ways of protecting what you've achieved. It's also a time for you to wash away the cobwebs and begin choosing new goals. After all, if you're not moving forward, you're stagnating or even losing ground. If you're not growing you're decaying.

The Waning Moon is marked by the opening up of your mind to the new possibilities represented by the goals you've just set. You can release all responsibility about the decisions you've been thinking about. Now is the time to begin to move forward once again, drawing upon positive emotions only, and letting go of everything else.

I'm a great listener. For personal assistance through coaching, please contact **me@wilmadavidaguila.com**.

MENTAL ATTITUDE

Mental attitude is everything. How can I say this? Well, science has shown that the mind cannot tell the difference between what is clearly imagined and what is real. This is the reason why memory is subjective. It's also the reason why two people who have had the exact same experience may produce conflicting reports about the experience. What does this have to do with drug abuse? Using the concept just described, you can actually imagine yourself well! You see, whatever the mind of man can conceive, it can achieve. No truer statement was ever uttered. If you can see a thing in your mind, like a clear photograph, then you can achieve it. Your mind can't tell that it isn't real. Therefore, when you tell it to attain that clear picture, it will take you out into the world to find or create it.

New Moon: set that intention. Use questions like, "Can you build this for me?" When you get a "Yes," tell your mind to do it, to make it happen. It will listen and obey.

Waxing Moon: use your mind to transform the world and your life. Build something that never existed before you came along, or build a better mousetrap. Your mind is your secret ally.

Full Moon: Take what you have managed to do and protect it to the best of your ability, then rest and prepare to begin anew.

Waning Moon: Let your mind soar. Envision the possibilities as clearly as you possibly can. Prepare for taking new actions.

The topic of mental attitude also relates to one of the most important laws of the universe, the Law of Attraction. This law explains the impact of mental attitude. The Law of Attraction states that we will attract into our lives whatever we are focusing on. It is easy to be unaware of the impact it can have on our lives. Either knowingly or unknowingly, a person sends out thoughts and emotions and attracts back like a magnet more of what they have put out. If you leave your thoughts, emotions and actions unchecked it is easy to attract unwanted things in your life. However, there is also great potential locked within you, and if you apply the Law of Attraction in your life you can encourage the universe to give you great things.

One of the worst parts of misusing drugs is that the artificial feeling you can get from them encourages you to want to use them again to get the relief they give. This signals to the universe that you need more of the drug(s), and that is what the universe will return to you. The same occurs with misinterpreting medical health problems. The more you think you have a health issue, the more the universe tells you that you do. The opposite happens if you believe you can get better, or that you can stop using drugs. The universe will send positive signs, and as your health and lack of dependency improves you will receive more and more benefit from the universe. Focusing on your drug dependency brings more dependency, but focusing on the good in your life brings more good.

When you start sending the right signals into the universe, you have started the New Moon phase. Set your new intentions and welcome positive change. It is a new beginning. As the universe starts to return what you have requested due to the Law of Attraction, the Waxing Moon is in phase and the transformation begins. As your wishes and goals become true, you have harvested what the Law of Attraction and the universe have given you, and the phase reaches a Full Moon. Next the Waning Moon is upon you, and you let go, open up and think of the next thing you want to attract from the universe.

I can help you create more useful attitudes. For personal assistance through coaching, please contact **me@wilmadavidaguila.com**.

REACTIONS

Misinterpreted health issues and the drugs that follow rarely occur spontaneously. They are generally a reaction to something else. To get to the root of this you must inspect your life and find what is root of the reaction(s) that has led you to where you are. What is the stressor that is making you feel health affects and/or leading you to turn to self-medication?

Stress is an inevitable part of life, and completely normal. However, left unchecked it can wreak havoc on your life and happiness. It may arise from something as simple as traffic, an important meeting, or increased work load at the office. It can also be severe and prolonged, such as the stress experienced by those who have faced or still face emotional or physical abuse. When overwhelmed by stress, you may feel defeated, and this inability to cope may lead you to turn to unhealthy solutions such as drug abuse.

Not only is stress troubling in itself, but it can have real physical effects on your body. Physical symptoms can be vast, and commonly include increased heart rate, nausea, dizziness and digestive problems. What you thought had been ailing you may not be the physical illness you found in a book or on the internet, but actually a result of unchecked stress in your life. You may be surprised that some of the physical symptoms you face are healed by simply finding and resolving the source of your stress.

Deciding to find what causes your reactions is a huge first step in overcoming the issues you face. In the New Moon phase, you need to decide to make positive changes in your life. Your intention needs to be focused on finding out the cause of your problems and channeling your reactions in a beneficial way. During the Waxing Moon phase, you will grow and learn about yourself. Once you have identified what causes your reactions, you can transform those reactions into ones that heal you instead of just hiding your problems. As you feel the cleansing effect of constructive reactions you can begin to heal, and during this period you will be under the phase of the Full Moon. You will soon be able to open up, let go and release the baggage of your negative reaction (the Waning Moon).

For personal assistance through coaching, please contact me@wilmadavidaguila.com.

AFTERTASTE

When you first turn to drug misuse to solve your problems, they seem sweet. They appear to help you. You might even feel that your life has improved. What you will soon notice, though, is that drugs do not come without a bitter aftertaste. Focusing on this aftertaste is something you can use to motivate yourself to stop drugs and improve your life.

The New Moon phase is the perfect time to recognize the bitter aftertaste drug misuse leaves in your life. It is a time to learn that the drug may not be helping you as much as it seems, and may actually be bringing negativity into your life. It is the time to start on the journey of truly measuring the cons of your use.

As you learn more about the aftertaste of drug misuse, you enter the phase of the Waxing Moon. Your perception starts to grow and your view transforms from only seeing the positives of the drug to understanding that it also introduces negatives. This is an important step in the healing process.

At some point you will realize the drug misuse is just not worth it. This is the phase of the Full Moon. It is a cleansing experience, and the point where you see the drug for the burden that it is. As the Waning Moon phase begins, you let go of your dependency on the drug and open yourself up to a life free of the drugs influence.

I can help you beat your drug problem. Please contact me@wilmadavidaguila.com.

COPING

When someone is no longer able to cope with the stresses of life, they begin to look elsewhere for crutches to help keep up, or reasons to explain their failure to cope. Untreated chronic stress can lead to serious health conditions. These conditions include anxiety, insomnia, muscle pain, high blood pressure and a weakened immune system. This explains why some people improperly self-diagnose medical issues and turn to drugs for self-medication. It is important to realize when you begin to no longer be able to keep up and cope with life issues. Learning to cope with stress in healthy ways is an important aspect of a successful life.

Learning to manage stress in a healthy way, when it occurs, can mitigate many of the negative health effects it can cause. People are diverse and different and, thus, so are the ways they can deal with stress. Some people enjoy pursuing hobbies such as team sports, music and art, while others enjoy more solitary activities like meditation, walking and yoga.

I've listed below five healing techniques to help reduce both short and long term success...

1. Take a break from the stressor

It may seem difficult to step away from things like an important work project or a sick child, but when you allow yourself to do so there are many benefits. By giving yourself permission to have space from your stressor you gain the opportunity to do something else, and this in turn allows you to have a new perspective and practice techniques which make you feel less overwhelmed. This doesn't mean avoiding your stress completely, but even a twenty-minute break to take care of yourself can be extremely helpful.

2. Exercise

Everyday more and more research shows that exercise benefits not just the body but also the mind. While most of us know the long-term benefits of exercise, there are also short-term benefits. A quick 20-minute workout or physical activity during a stressful time can rejuvenate you, and improve your focus. This effect is almost immediate and can last for several hours.

3. Smile and laugh

Your emotions and facial expression can send feedback to the brain and have a direct effect on its function. When we are stressed we often hold much of this stress in our faces. Smiling and laughing is an effective way to relieve some of this tension and can improve the situation by signalling to your brain things are not so bad after all.

4. Get social support

If you feel overwhelmed, do not forget you can always call a friend or send someone you trust an email. Sharing your concerns with another person can help relieve your stress. However, trust is important, and you need to know the person will understand and can validate you. If your family is a stressor it may not help to share your work woes with them, and you may be better off calling a close friend.

5. Meditate

One of the best ways to help the mind and body focus and relax is to practice meditation or mindful prayer. The mindfulness that arises from this is a powerful tool to help you see new perspectives, and develop self-compassion and forgiveness. The process allows you to release emotion which may have been causing your body to experience physical stress. Just like exercise research has shown to relieve stress, a brief period of meditation can bring immediate benefits.

The moon phase can help you tackle stress effectively. Identify your stressor and plan how to relieve your stress. This can be thought of as the phase of the New Moon. As you implement your coping mechanisms and your stress begins to release, you are under the Waxing Moon. The Full Moon will signal you can cope with the stressor, and you can face and complete the tasks causing you stress under the Waning Moon without fear.

For coaching in coping and lifestyle skills, please contact **me@wilmadavidaguila.com**.

SIDE EFFECTS

One of the biggest issues with self-diagnosis and drug misuse is that people often only target the side effect. As mentioned before, stress can cause physical problems. Dealing with the physical problems may work temporarily, but the original issues remain. While drugs may make you feel okay, the true problem may still be growing under that shroud you have created, waiting for the right opportunity to reappear and wreak havoc on your life.

Don't assume the issues you face are the only problem. The New Moon is the phase of your life to search for things that may be causing the problems you face. Instead of tackling multiple problems individually and ending up leaving the root cause not dealt with, attack the issue at its source and deal with all the side effects simultaneously. Is your lack of sleep due to a medical issue or is it from the stress of taking on too much at work?

During the Waxing Moon you will discover the truth about your issues, you can learn about how the problems you face arose, and you can begin to heal yourself of your issues. Taking the previous example, you may choose to delegate some of the work. Your sleep might start to improve and you may notice you no longer need those sleeping pills. Additionally, you may see other side effects that you may have missed or linked to another problem. Now that you are not so tired you find yourself helping with the cleaning (for example) and causing less conflict with your spouse. These effects will leave you harvesting the benefits of the Full Moon. Once these side effects have stabilized you will experience the Waning Moon, and can open yourself up to new challenges and let go of the problems of your past.

For someone to listen and to coach you through your stress issues, please contact **me@wilmadavidaguila.com**.

METAPHYSICAL

Drug misuse isn't only related to physical issues but is deeply connected to the metaphysical nature of a person's being. Drug use can be looked at through a spiritual lens. Spirituality refers to belief in a power greater that oneself. One which governs the universe and has a sense of interconnectedness with all living things. It may also involve a quest for self-knowledge, meaning and purpose in one's life. Using drugs is a way to detach and disconnect from the present moment, and all the uncomfortable feelings that go with it. Drug misuse and addiction can also be thought of as having an isolating effect, one that can arise from a lack of connection to one's authentic self, a higher power or persons in the larger community.

Approaching the problems of drug misuse from a spiritual and metaphysical standpoint can be very effective.

One way to approach this is a metaphysical take on the 12 steps, from Ester Nicholson's book *Soul Recovery: The 12 Keys to Healing Addiction*:

1. You are the Power: Through my conscious union with the infinite universal presence, I am powerful, clear and free. Through the realization that God is within me, expressing as me, my life is in divine and perfect order.

2. Restored to wholeness: Through my conscious connection with the one power, I reclaim my spiritual dominion and emotional balance. I am restored to my original nature of clarity, peace and wholeness. I am restored.

3. Complete surrender: I turn my life over to the care of the God I understand, know and embody as love, harmony, peace, health, prosperity and joy. I know that which I am surrendering to, and I do so absolutely. Knowing that this power is the very essence of my being, I say with my whole heart and mind: Thy will be done.

4. An examined life: Through my absolute surrender and conscious connection to the one power and presence, I courageously, deeply and gently search within myself for all thought patterns and behaviours that are out of alignment with love, integrity, harmony and order.

5. Living out loud: I claim the courage and willingness to share the exact nature of my mistakes with another spiritual being. I am heard with compassion, unconditional love and wisdom. In this loving vibration, clarity, peace and balance are restored.

6. Honouring the inner child: I am now ready to release all thought patterns and behaviors unlike my true nature, which is wholeness. I free-fall into the loving presence of spirit within, and allow it to heal every known and unknown false belief. I am transformed by the renewal of my mind.

7. Never give up: In loving compassion for every aspect of my being, I humbly surrender to the love of spirit. I know myself as a perfect expression of life. I surrender all, and I am restored to the life I am created to live.

8. Willingness: I acknowledge the people I have offended based on false beliefs, fear, doubt and unworthiness. I am willing to go to any lengths to clean up my side of the street.

9. Cleaning up the wreckage: Backed by all the power of the universe, I lovingly, directly and honestly make amends in a way that supports the highest good of all concerned.

10. Spiritual maintenance: I am in tune with my inner self. With integrity, love and self-compassion, I acknowledge my mistakes and continue to clean up the mistakes of my past and present.

11. Conscious contact: Through daily prayer and meditation, I deepen my conscious connection to the divine and experience the fullness of the universal presence as the dynamic reality of my life.

12. Loving service: Through my awakened consciousness, I am now prepared to carry the message of truth out into the world. I am now a clear channel to support the awakening of others to their true identity of wholeness.

The 12 keys or steps also span the phases of the moon. Steps one to four represent the New Moon. Steps five to eight represent the Waxing Moon. Steps nine to 11 represent the Full Moon. And the last step, 12, represents the Waxing Moon.

For spiritual and metaphysical coaching, please contact me@wilmadavidaguila.com.

VIBRATION

Vibration is your energetic resonance, and it represents how you think, feel and act. It is the energy the attracts every experience in your life. To ensure happiness and attract good things in your life you want to have positive vibrations. Keeping your vibrations positive will attract positive thoughts and in turn create positive experiences that will match the vibrations of health and abundance. Being in this state is a requirement to attract that which you want.

Dark energies and entities will weaken you and lower your vibrations. Drugs may be a choice you make to try to remedy the state you feel yourself falling into. Drug misuse may trick you into thinking you are improving but actually can bring your vibrations even lower and make a positive state even harder to achieve. Instead of drug misuse you should look into ways to raise your vibration and attract positive energy.

I've included ten steps that can help you raise your vibrations and move away from the vibration lowering temptation of drug misuse:

1. When situations or people drag you down, distance yourself from them so your vibrations are not affected by the negative energy.

2. Raise your energy and awareness by refocusing through daily meditation.

3. A warm bath with Epsom salts and a couple drops of essential oils can help you grow your vibrational energy.

4. Deep breathing is a good way to bring oxygen to your brain and blood stream, and allow your energy to resonate in a positive fashion.

5. Avoid the polluting effect of the toxins from unnecessary drugs, alcohol and nicotine.

6. Find ways to exercise creativity through things like art, poetry, writing or photography.

7. Say what you are grateful for out loud to help grow those vibrations.

8. Be kind to others in your daily activities, and genuinely smile to attract more of the positive energy that comes from it.

9. Exercising at least once a day can deplete negative energy and build positive vibrations.

10. Keeping hydrated keeps your body running efficiently and allows your vibrational level to stay stable.

In the New Moon stage, you need to focus on positive energy and the state of your vibrations. The Waxing Moon is where you will grow your vibrations by focusing on your health and creative outlets. As your vibrations grow you will transition into the Full Moon period and you will feel healing energy, and may even notice transformations beginning in your life. The benefits will start to become apparent as your new vibrational state stabilizes. This signifies the New Moon phase, and many new opportunities will become apparent. As you open yourself up to new energies and let go of negative energy in your life during the Waning Moon, you can prepare for bringing your vibrations to even greater levels.

For personal assistance with building up your energy levels, please contact me@wilmadavidaguila.com.

AWAKENING

When you begin to put the lessons from all the previous sections together, you will awaken to the idea that your personal issues or health problems are not always served by drugs. This point is the beginning of the overarching New Moon. It may take you many moon cycles to reach this place. As you learn to release all the various problems through past Waning Moons, accept that the issues you face can be fixed as you surrender yourself to the universe and all the good it can bring you. This Waxing Moon will bring immense growth and overall healing. You will transform into the best version your current self has experienced. The Full Moon will cleanse you and your wish for a life free of drug misuse will come true. The next Waning Moon will allow you open yourself up to all the potential that was already there but that you had not been able to see.

For personal assistance through coaching or for group seminars, please contact **me@wilmadavidaguila.com**.

Single Again?

Wealth Planning On One Income

LINDA J. LEVESQUE CFP, FCSI

Yesterday is gone, tomorrow has not yet come.
We only have today, let us begin.
— Mother Teresa

As of this moment, I have spent over twenty-three years working as a financial planner. Over the course of my career, I have had multiple clients who sought guidance after being widowed or separated or who were going through a divorce. In fact, I have been through two separations myself. Although my husband and I never divorced, we went through the process of separating our assets twice because we had tried working it out to no avail. Thus, I can safely say that I know firsthand how difficult and expensive the process can be.

Losing your lifelong partner to death or through divorce can be stressful, scary, and even traumatic. Financially you may feel overwhelmed, lost and in desperate need of some guidance, especially if your partner made most of the financial decisions. This is perfectly understandable as the transition from planning on two incomes to planning on one is seldom an easy change to make. Nevertheless, it is an evolution for which you have to prepare.

Additionally, if you never worried about saving because you had two incomes that together afforded you a certain lifestyle, you may have to learn how to budget and save. You may even need to make adjustments to your way of living. This might mean learning to "pay you" first (into savings). You will definitely need to teach yourself to handle all the finances, shopping and budget management, things that you may have relied on your partner for in the past. This will inevitably be a major turning point in your life, but the better informed and prepared you are, the easier it will be to confront it.

DIVORCE/SEPARATION

There is absolutely no doubt that divorce itself can be costly, especially in a modern context. In most cases, both parties can lose substantial amounts of money to legal fees — it is not unheard of to spend up to $200,000. Plus, if you are trying to win custody of your children, there could be no cost ceiling on legal fees.

In order to keep yourself from becoming financially ruined, you need to take stock of your whole situation. This includes what money you currently have in your name that you have access to; where you are planning to live and what your net wealth was when you were married versus what it will be after your divorce is finalized. Will you be able to stay in the family home or will you have to move? The cost of setting up house somewhere else in a lifestyle you and/or your children have become accustomed to may be a big adjustment when living on a single income.

In the beginning of your breakup, it is easy to get in the hole financially very quickly, especially with increasing legal fees. That is why it is important to pick your battles carefully. If you don't, your lawyers could end up walking away with the lion's share of your money, your children's college fund, your retirement savings, the equity in your home, etc. You get the picture. Be very wary. Lawyers have every incentive to encourage acrimony rather than strive to reduce conflict.

My colleague went through a divorce several years ago. After $200,000 in legal fees, he finally had to say enough is enough and, unfortunately, he still does not have access to his children. What he learned from the process was that you need to pick your battles. Every time you have a problem with your ex you cannot run to the telephone and call your lawyer. Of course, the lawyer does not mind because they will bill you in increments at several hundred dollars an hour. But, you should care, because what this does could deplete your pool of cash. You need to document and save up your questions and concerns for the lawyer so you can deal with several issues at a time. You should also learn to tell the difference between a real issue and something you are just upset about. Otherwise, you could end up paying for something that will never get resolved in the legal system.

My ex-husband had to learn this the hard way when we were going through our separation the first time. Because I was the one who wanted out of the marriage, he felt that I should not get a fair split on the matrimonial assets. I had worked all through our marriage (not that it should matter when splitting your assets). In any event, at one point during the negotiations my ex refused to give me half of our assets. "Fine," I said. "We'll go to the lawyers, and they'll get their share. We'll end up with about 25% of our estate each, and they'll get 50%. They'll be laughing all the way to the bank."

Since my ex did not like to waste money, and he knew I would go all the way with this (and he would have ended up with a lot less), he finally agreed that we both were entitled to half of what we owned. We did not have children to fight about, so this experience ended up very amicable in the end and, to this day, my ex-husband still trusts me to manage his finances.

In another situation, before I was an advisor I met a man who was going through a divorce. We will call him Joe. Joe felt guilty that he was leaving his second wife and her children. Joe wanted to make it easy on his conscience, so he was going to give his ex-wife everything they had built up together over the ten years of their marriage.

I was friends with Joe, and explained that he needed his fair share in order to start over. During the ten years of marriage, Joe had spent a good deal of time helping raise his wife's children, so she could go back to school and get a higher paying job than he had. I told Joe that, when the dust settled, he would regret giving everything away and starting over in his 40's. Joe gave the majority of his matrimonial assets to his ex-wife but took enough to get a down payment on a new home so he could move on. The split was amicable and never had to involve the lawyers except to process the actual divorce. This situation does not happen so easily most of the time.

When I became an investment advisor in 1990, Joe called me up and starting investing with me because he had listened to my advice. He had never forgotten what an impact it made on his financial life.

Even before I realized my calling to become an investment advisor, I understood the importance of looking at the big picture if you want to enjoy a certain financial lifestyle. Getting into this business allowed me to more formally guide people, helping them get past the hurt of divorce and look at the financial impact that needs to be addressed.

ONE STEP BACKWARD

In the midst of the conflict, you may be forced to sell your house and move back in with your parents — if this option is even available. This could have a harmful effect on your sense of self-respect and independence. But know that, if such a thing happens, you have to look at it as a temporary setback. Remember, "This too shall pass."

Maybe you will never have all that you had before. And, yes, your lifestyle may have to be adjusted, but this is okay because it only means you may be going back to the basics. This is not the end of the world but a challenge to the person you are. When you work with a good investment advisor, they will help you reach your financial goals again. And, those goals will now be your goals, and you get to make all the decisions about how you want your financial future to look. If you have children, they will eventually leave, and your retirement and lifestyle goals become what is important to you. You may lack the finances to get started again on your own, but in due time you begin a new chapter of your life.

A SENSE OF LOSS

After being separated, divorced or widowed from your mate, you may feel a sense of emptiness or a void welling inside you where the love of your life used to be. (Of course, you may also feel a sense of relief or freedom. That too is normal.) As such, it can be tempting to try to fill that void by making an immediate return to the dating scene. This is usually a mistake, and it can often end in failure. In fact, a survey conducted by the Forest Institute of Professional Psychology revealed that 67% of second marriages end in divorce.

You should not start dating again until you are emotionally ready. Ask yourself if you've truly separated yourself from your old partner; not just legally, but emotionally — and be prepared to give yourself an honest answer. A signed document legitimizing your 'divorced' status means only so much, after all.

And don't let the experience of separation damage your self-esteem or sense of worth. You may start to feel unattractive, unworthy or even abnormal in the wake of a divorce. This is absolutely normal, especially if you were not the one that initiated the split. At this very moment, millions of adults across the continent are going through the exact trials and tribulations that you're going through. Remember that you're not alone.

I find that, when you join a support group and are surrounded by people that share similar life events, you make smarter personal and financial decisions. Again, working with an experienced advisor will sometimes help save you from yourself both emotionally and financially. Even though dating should be out for the first year or so, you still need to go out and socialize. You can start by joining a health club, gym or emotional support group — any kind of social gathering, really — so that you can start connecting with other people as soon as you feel comfortable doing so.

Living, working and planning your finances on one income may not be as bad as you imagine it will be once you take full control of your financial decisions. Remember you are not alone. What you don't want is to allow the experience of being separated, divorced or widowed to overtake your life in a negative way. Even though the thought of going through life on your own may seem daunting, having your close friends and family near you will help you move forward. Your relationships with people you trust will help prevent you from making unnecessary financial and/or health decisions.

DEATH

Joyce, a friend of mine, lost her husband to cancer about ten years ago. My friend's husband had battled cancer for approximately three years before he finally passed away. When everything was said and done, my friend went on a spending spree. (I had met her after her husband had already passed away.)

Joyce was in her mid-fifties at the time she was widowed. She did not have any close family or friends nearby, and she had two adult children who lived far away. After the funeral, her children left, and Joyce was on her own. You always hope your family and friends will stand by you; they are the ones you expect to rely on through thick and thin.

Not only did Joyce lose her husband, but she was forced to close her business during an economic downturn shortly thereafter. One of the things that happen quite often to divorced and widowed people is that they make major financial decisions before they are emotionally ready to think straight. Joyce was in that category.

Anyway, because Joyce was very alone, and had abandoned a lot of her friends during the time she nursed her sick husband, she needed an outlet. Joyce wanted to change her whole life and leave everything behind from her past. She decided to sell her matrimonial home; in doing so, she gave away almost everything that she had shared with her husband. Joyce did not want to be reminded of the life she had and would no longer have. She could have sold stuff and kept the cash for a time in the future when she would need it. But, being grief struck, with no one to guide her or provide a shoulder to lean on, Joyce gave away valuable tools, a car and furniture to anyone who had been at all kind to her. Joyce would have benefited from grief counseling to help her adjust to her new life. Joyce also did not have the financial advice that she had during her husband's life because her advisor had retired and the son that took over did not have the relationship or experience to help my friend out.

So, because my friend (who was a very new friend to me) wanted to remake herself, she started spending money like there was no tomorrow. In Joyce's mind, there was no tomorrow. Joyce's husband died so very young, and the plans of a happy retirement together was no longer an option. Joyce sold the family home and purchased a new, smaller and more manageable home. This would have been a good decision had Joyce not freed up money to spend on frivolous purchases, only to find herself ten years later watching every penny. Joyce furnished the whole house with new furniture, purchased a new car, and constantly shopped for new clothes for all the many vacations she started to take. Oh and I forgot to mention that Joyce also took up a new hobby, gambling.

Since Joyce had not started to date, and she did not have a lot of close friends, she found herself going out to the casino to play the slots. Joyce said it gave her something to do, and she was around people, so it made her feel she was not alone. Joyce justified her gambling as entertainment, and she said she always stuck to a budget. Even if the budget was, in her words, modest — at approximately $300 for the evening— the amount soon became more than she could afford, especially once she added that entertainment to the clothes, vacations, furniture etc. that Joyce was always spending on.

Joyce soon came to the realization that she might live a lot longer than she had thought. The good thing that Joyce always did, and continues to do is belong to a gym where she exercises on a regular basis. Joyce maintains a healthy lifestyle and now has a goal of living to a ripe old age. It is too bad that I did not know Joyce well enough at the time she was going crazy spending. I may have been able to show her the light and the potential lifestyle she could have been enjoying. Even though Joyce has made a lot of financial mistakes, she looks back and says she is still very fortunate to have what she has so she will not live with regret. I wish I could have been there then. I am here for Joyce today, but all I can do is keep helping her understand the difference between needs and wants now that she has to plan on one income.

As a side note, if you have minor children, you may want to consider getting counseling for them. You may think that they've adjusted, but it would be beneficial for your children to have a third party they can talk to, someone who can evaluate their mental state objectively. Joyce could have used counseling; she thought she was fine, but could not control her emotional spending. Children can appear okay, but have their "outlet" come out somewhere else later. Luckily Joyce's children were already adults and living apart. Joyce really never knew how her children's decisions were impacted by their father's death.

PLANNING

Careful financial planning is essential. The worst thing you can do when living on one income is to let impulses take over. You are going to make the transition from planning on two incomes to planning on one income, and you must adjust accordingly. That means paying yourself first and adjusting your spending accordingly. It means deciding when you want to retire and making sure that you'll be able to afford to live in the retirement lifestyle of your choice. More importantly, it means creating your own budget. Remember, you will be living on one income, not two, so you're going to be solely responsible for all of the money that comes in and all of the money that goes out.

Having an advisor to discuss budgeting and cash flow should help keep the spending to a minimum. I know a lot of people, and they still shop for groceries as if they were cooking for two or more, then throwing out food because they could not eat it all. It happens when you are used to being a couple and keeping the pantry well stocked but, once alone, find yourself calling up friends and eating out more often. Again, a lot of food goes to waste, and that waste is like throwing out money. You need to think about how you are affected by living on one income.

If you are widowed, and continue to live in the family home, you need to consider that your reduced income may make keeping up the family home financially difficult. There are things to be dealt with, such as insurance, transferring existing assets to your name, learning about what government benefits you can apply for and, of course, estate planning for your eventual demise. These are things you can discuss with your financial advisor so as to keep you on the right track.

If you are divorced or separated, there are questions to be asked and things to be considered:

- How will the assets be split, including investments and bank accounts?
- How do you budget on one income?
- What cash flow will you be working with?

- Will you get child and/or spousal support?
- Are there any government benefits you qualify for?
- What insurances will be needed and what changes should be made to life, disability and critical illness insurances? Do you need to name new beneficiaries on your existing plans?
- How will taxation be affected?
- What do you need to consider in terms of your new estate plan, will and powers of attorney?

As daunting as this may seem, these responsibilities can be manageable if you follow some simple guidelines. Having someone you trust to discuss major financial decisions with will be a big help in not getting your finances derailed. First and foremost, never try to make big financial decisions in the first year after becoming widowed. Take some time to settle down and find out what you have and what you need.

If your spouse left you some money in the form of a pension plan, make sure that you know what your options are in regards to what you can do with it. Also, if you get a large sum of money from an insurance policy, you may want to talk with a trusted financial advisor to discuss the best way to use the insurance to supplement your income (so you can continue living the lifestyle of your choice).

Sometimes, when people inherit a large insurance policy, they look at it as a win fall. They start spending money foolishly, or give a lot of it away without any thought as to how doing so may impact their future. I have seen situations where adult children started coming around and asking to borrow some money without ever having the intention of paying it back. My advice would be not to have the money too accessible. Instead of leaving it in a personal bank account, (not much in the way of interest at this point anyway), using a qualified trusted investment advisor can reap you big rewards in managing the big picture of planning.

A trusted qualified advisor will draft a wealth plan taking into consideration all aspects of your financial life. The advisor will clarify your situation, discuss your personal and financial goals, help identify some of the challenges you may have, provide a written plan, help to execute the plan and then do regular checkups in case things have changed or the plan needs to be tweaked. All of this will help give you peace of mind when you are faced with so many decisions on your own and planning on one income.

When you need money you can have your advisor deposit directly to your bank account. Having to call your advisor for money gives you the opportunity to have a cooling off period if need be. Or, when someone wants to borrow money, you have the excuse of saying your money is tied up. Your advisor can be a big savior from people hounding you for money or if you are an impulse shopper.

CHOOSING A FINANCIAL ADVISOR

So, you may be wondering how you can choose a reputable financial advisor, especially as choosing which financial advisor to hire can be tricky. Usually, the best place to start is to have someone referred to you, someone with whom your friends and relatives are happy. Ideally, the person you choose should be someone you can establish a personal bond with, someone you'll feel comfortable with seeing on a regular basis over a long period of time and you can be open with.

Often I get clients saying they were with another advisor, but they sometimes felt intimidated by them. Clients did not understand what the advisor was saying because it was not phrased in simple everyday terms. Clients would often feel inadequate to make a decision, so a lot of times, would not make any decision for fear of making the wrong one. You need someone who can reliably guide you in the right direction and do so in a language you can understand.

For obvious reasons, you are going to want someone with experience and education in the area of financial planning. If the advisor has a designation such as a CFP (Certified Financial Planner), you know that the person takes their career seriously. Remember, anyone can sell you products. The advisor you choose is someone to whom you will make a commitment for the better part of your life. As an advisor myself (for over twenty-three years), I have clients I met at the beginning of my career who have become friends. I have seen them marry, have children and, of course, sometimes divorce or become widowed. I have helped a lot of people with all aspects of their financial life.

For this reason and others I've mentioned, you need to have someone you can trust, someone who will view you as a friend as well as a client. After hearing my recommendations, a lot of my clients say, "What would you do if this were your money?" Or, "would you invest your mother's money in this?" You have to feel as if you matter. You have to feel as if you are being heard. What you are communicating to the advisor is also what is considered in the plan. Your wealth plan is a two way street with feedback from you and from the advisor. You may have to interview several advisors before you select one. Don't feel pressured or intimidated by anyone. Remember this is your money. This is your financial future.

Another point you may want to consider when seeking out a trusted financial advisor is whether that person works for a reputable company. Having said that, I know you can still meet unscrupulous advisors. This is why referrals are usually a good place to start. I work for a company whose policy is that you work for the client. If you do something deliberately that is not in their best interest, then my company will hang you out to dry. If you make a mistake, then it helps you to correct that mistake. You want a company who tries to hire only the most ethical people those who will not bring embarrassment to the company.

Today, with the Internet, you can google a company and get a lot of information on the firm. You want one that will stand by your side if your advisor lets you down. A company and advisor that receive referrals and continuing patronage from a diverse body of clients are, generally speaking, a safer bet. This is also part of the reason why the interview process is so vital; any credible planner will be willing to hold an introductory meeting free of charge.

All the same, though, you are probably not going to want a financial planner who works for a company that is too small or underemployed. This is not to say that small companies are necessarily bad, far from it. The problem is that they are less likely than bigger ones to be able to cater to your needs at any given time. If your financial planner works for a "one man shop," so to speak, then you will be dependent on their availability. If the advisor happens to be out sick, or on vacation, you will be left with nobody to answer your questions. In certain situations, this can be extremely problematic.

Not all financial planners have the same area of expertise, so it is important to find the one best suited to your current financial situation. In general, your financial planner should also be committed to observing the bigger economic picture. Having an advisor looking at the macro picture and keeping up with market trends can be beneficial in long term planning. Short term goals should be in short term investments and your advisor should understand the difference.

As a financial planner, I recognize the importance of keeping tabs on what's going on in the market so that I can help my clients determine where they see themselves wanting to go and what lifestyle they want to live. So should yours.

By no means is it going to be easy to begin this new stage/chapter of your life. You don't have to be afraid, but you do have to be cautious. Finding the right advisor can help planning on one income less daunting.

Ask others for help as well. Hire a lawyer and an accountant, along with a financial advisor, to assist you in this complex process — especially when you may still be very emotional. For more information about the financial considerations associated with living on your own, please visit **www.levesquetelmossewealthplanning.com**. Also, you may find the book Single Again, Wealth Planning on One Income, very helpful.

Linda J. Levesque CFP®, FCSI
Director, Private Client Group
HollisWealth (a division of Scotia Capital Inc.)

Bringing Balance to Your Life

DENNIS GARRIDO

When I woke up in the hospital staring up into the terrified eyes of someone I cared about, after my second cardiac arrest in one year, I knew that things had to change in my life. Especially because I was only in my twenties at the time.

Everything in my life was out of balance. Obviously, physically because I was lying in the emergency room, but more importantly my mind, emotions, and spirit were completely out of whack, and that had taken a toll on my body.

Now you may be wondering how someone so young could have had two cardiac arrests before the age of 30? It won't be hard to imagine once I share my story with you. I wish I could tell you that I had a great upbringing, one filled with laughter and love, but it wasn't.

At age eleven I was removed from my parent's home by The Children's Aid Society because they deemed my parents unfit to raise me. During that time, I went through a whirlwind of emotions. A part of me was happy that change was finally occurring, because clearly at that point, the way things were, wasn't working at all.

Another part of me felt fear because of the unknown. I didn't know exactly where I would be living, nor did I know for sure what my group & foster homes would be like, what the other kids would be like, what the living conditions would be like, how far or close I'd be to my family and hometown, etc. Essentially, I wasn't 100% certain nor 100% convinced that I was going into better circumstances.

Also, I felt sad, since I wouldn't see my parents or siblings anymore, nor my home town and many of the people whom I'd see on a regular basis; everything FAMILIAR would be gone! Lastly, I felt angry, that it had come to me being removed from my parent's house, away from those who were in my life for all those years. As twisted and messed up as it may be, I was angry that I was leaving a life that I had become accustomed to and felt somewhat comfortable in (comfortable in comparison to the unknown that lay ahead); and most of all, angry that I was leaving FAMILIARITY!!!!

Please understand me, I am no longer angry at my parents, and you shouldn't be either. They did the best they could, but when you are broken yourself, unless you find a way out, you will repeat what had been bestowed on you from the previous generations. I can be thankful because what I went through helped create the person I am today and as a coach, it gives me great empathy and understanding to be able to help others. So, don't feel sorry for me because even though my life had a rough start, I get to choose the rest of it and it is going to be GREAT!!!

THE NEXT SEVEN YEARS OF MY LIFE

For the next seven years until I turned 18, I was bounced from foster/group home to foster/group home. I rarely spent more than three months at any one place, and it caused some major emotional setbacks that took me a long time to overcome.

One of the biggest negative emotional setbacks was again to do with familiarity. As I spent time with those at my new home, seeing them every day and coming to know them personally; I naturally formed a connection/friendship with them. It seemed that no sooner had I done that; they were removed from my life. People whom I really liked (a few of them, whom I loved), ALL GONE!!! Which basically solidified my already ingrained defence mechanism of keeping distant from others; not allowing anyone to get close enough to form any connection with me.

Inevitably, this made it very difficult for me to form any type of relationship with anyone. School and extracurricular activities were hard because I never knew how long I would be staying in one place. What was the point of making friends if I could never keep them? It was a lot easier to keep my distance than to reach out yet again and have everything torn away from me.

Eventually, I started to tear down the wall that prevented me from getting too close to anyone. To this day, the negative emotional setbacks I experienced, still affect me to some degree; though I CHOOSE not to allow them to prevent me from forming meaningful relationships!

THE DARKEST TIME OF MY LIFE

All that change led to one of the darkest periods of my life. Emotionally and mentally I had shut down and could no longer function. Life was so hard. Even things that were simple, now became agonizingly difficult and it hit the point where I didn't want to live anymore. What was the use of carrying on in this horrible life when there wasn't any hope of it changing?

My life began to narrow down to one permanent solution, and that was to end it all by committing suicide. I just couldn't handle life anymore, but I truly believe that Almighty God, the universe or whatever you want to call it, had a bigger plan for me. Even though I tried several times, I just couldn't die!!! Because of those attempts, I ended up in psychiatric institutions, a few times.

It finally came to the point where I was tired of trying to die, I was tired of institutions and I was weary from all the self-harm, and so I came to a decision. I guess you could say that it was a turning point in my life; I wasn't going to attempt suicide anymore. I wasn't sure what to do because my circumstances hadn't changed, but I was willing to look for options. That was the beginning point of change in my life. The will to live!!!

IT DIDN'T GET BETTER RIGHT AWAY

Life is a journey with twists, hills, and valleys of varying shapes and sizes, with occasional points where you make decisions that put you on a different path. The determination not to kill myself had set me on a new road, but I still didn't know what to do or which way to go. It was slow going as I fumbled my way through, but at least I was moving forward!!!

At age 18 I was no longer in the custody of The Children's Aid Society, so I moved back with my parents, which was the perfect testing grounds for me to apply the life lessons I had learned so far. You would be amazed by how much maturity one can have at 18 when you have been through what I have. It wasn't easy, and it was hard work, but I managed to re-establish a relationship with my parents and not only complete high school, but also graduate from post-secondary schooling.

One of the things I had decided to do was get my student loans paid off in the six-month grace period, which I managed to do; but in doing so, I pushed myself way beyond my physical limits which brought on the first cardiac arrest.

You would think I would have learned from that first experience, but I didn't, and less than a year later we are back to the beginning of this chapter waking up in the hospital from my second one.

This time I learned my lesson and chose a different path, but I still didn't know how to achieve what I needed. For so long I had lived in imbalance, that I didn't know where to start, but the catalyst for change was just around the corner.

I FINALLY REALIZED WHAT BALANCE WAS

Believe it or not, it is the simplest things that can bring about the most profound changes in life. My search for balance in my life had begun, and it is amazing how the answer came; by a knock at my door one day.

That day I was busy working on something, so when the first knock came, I ignored it. It was only after a couple of rings of the doorbell that I finally decided that I would answer it. There was a well-dressed gentleman at the door and even though I don't remember most of what he said, one thing became clear, I was missing an essential element to finding the balance I craved. Now, I knew what it was. You can only find balance when you address ALL the areas of your life, and I had been missing one. The spiritual side.

It is amazing what happens when you finally have all the pieces together. As I started to study the Bible, I finally could build a solid spiritual foundation, that enabled me to re-evaluate things in my life, and thus, put a plan together to create balance in my life. In the rest of this chapter, I am going to share with you what I learned.

Just before I do that, I do want to mention one thing. All of this is a process. Can I say that I am 100% balanced in my life? No, but when I started at 3-4% and then jumped to 85%, I think that is very good growth. It's difficult to attain 100% balance in every aspect of one's life, that is why even the most successful people keep learning and growing. So, the goal is not perfection, but growth. As long as you are continuing to move forward, that is all that matters.

7 STEPS TO BRING BALANCE TO YOUR LIFE

Here's one of the things that I have learned about bringing balance to your life. In some ways, it is easy. The steps I am going to teach you are simple to understand. The hard part is training yourself to be aware of it every day and live by it. The good thing is, though it may be hard at first, the more you practice it, the easier it gets.

STEP 1

Ask yourself, "What are my priorities in life?" You want to look at it from all aspects of your life, personal and professional. In terms of personal that includes goals physically, emotionally, mentally, spiritually, relationships (such as your spouse or significant other), family and friends. You want to look at it from the point of what you need and what you want. For each one, you should have one to two priorities.

In terms of professional, they can include your current work situation and areas of improvement there, plus plan for your future. Put down both needs and wants.

	NEEDS	WANTS
P E R S O N A L		
P R O F E S S I O N A L		

STEP 2

Look at your needs column. What are the most important priorities personally and professionally? It is important that you only start out working on a few at a time. If you try to do everything at once, you will become overwhelmed and quit. Then, figure out the things you need to do to get those needs met.

STEP 3

Now go through your wants and do the same thing as Step 2 above. Don't overlook this. Part of having balance in life is having both your needs and wants met. Obviously, your needs are more important, but without the wants, you give up hope.

STEP 4

Set up a timeline for those needs to be accomplished. What are you going to do today, this week, this month, this year, and in the next five years to bring yourself to reach those priorities?

STEP 5

Do the same thing for your wants. Set up your timeline of completion.

STEP 6

DO THE ACTIONS. Here is where the rubber meets the road. You can plan and plan and plan, but if there is no action involved you will be in the same place, with the same problems, five years from now.

STEP 7

Re-evaluate. Every few months go back through this whole process again.

As you grow and change, so will your priorities, your needs and your wants.

THE BEST WAY TO ACCOMPLISH THIS

Very rarely can a person accomplish this alone. Have you ever heard the saying, "You can't see the forest for the trees?" That is what happens in our lives. We get so caught up in the unimportant things right in front of us, that we miss the big picture and we don't recognize growth when it occurs.

Now, you do have several options. One is to have family members try to help you through this. While you do need their support, they are usually looking at the same trees you are and can miss things.

Two, you can go to friends for help. They do tend to see more of the big picture, but many times they can't give you the encouragement and motivation you need at times to get past yourself.

Three, you work with a professional who knows how to help you bring balance to your life. They can come alongside of you and guide you to the quickest path to success because there will be obstacles that try to stop you. Did I forget to mention that?

No road to balance is smooth; little pebbles will get into your shoes to irritate you and take your focus off your goals. Barriers will be put up that you will have to learn how to go over, under, around or through. People will get in your way and tell you that it is the wrong road to take and you should follow them. All sorts of things will try to keep you from what you want.

Coaches are keen observers who can not only help you with what is going on right now, but they have been down your road and they know what is up ahead and can keep you moving forward, even when everything is telling you to stop.

That is what I'm offering to be for you. Let me help you on your path to balance in your life. I have been on both sides of the coin, and I can guide you through the roughest parts. I can relate to what you are feeling and am more than willing to help you navigate this wonderful thing called life.

First of all, if you would like more information on how to start this process, you can pre-order my upcoming book at www.dennisgarrido.com Second, you can email me at dennis@dennisgarrido.com and request your free 15-minute phone consultation where we can discuss your situation and see if we are a good fit for each other. Third, maybe you realize more people need to hear this message. I am also available to speak to groups and conferences. If so, just send me an email, and we can arrange a time to speak.

No matter what you decide, know this. You can achieve balance in your life. It is possible. I can tell you that it has been worth everything I went through to get to this point. The peace I experience now, compared to the chaos I lived before, is so amazing and I wish the same for you.

Don't miss out. Make the choice to change your life today, and I guarantee that you won't regret it!!!

www.ingramcontent.com/pod-product-compliance
Lightning Source LLC
Chambersburg PA
CBHW050644160426
43194CB00010B/1796